D0602165

WITHDRAWN
BY
JEFFERSON COUNTY PUBLIC LIBRARY
Lakewood, CO

917.8 ANNERINO
Annerino, John.
Canyon country : a
photographic journey
sl
1142675702
JAN 2006

JEFFERSON CO PUBLIC LIB, CO

Canyon Country

Books by John Annerino

Photography

GRAND CANYON WILD
A Photographic Journey

ROUGHSTOCK
The Toughest Events in Rodeo

APACHE
The Sacred Path to Womanhood

PEOPLE OF LEGEND
Native Americans of the Southwest

THE WILD COUNTRY OF MEXICO
La tierra salvaje de México

CANYONS OF THE SOUTHWEST

HIGH RISK PHOTOGRAPHY
The Adventure Behind the Image

Also by the author

RUNNING WILD
An Extraordinary Adventure of the Human Spirit

DEAD IN THEIR TRACKS
Crossing America's Desert Borderlands

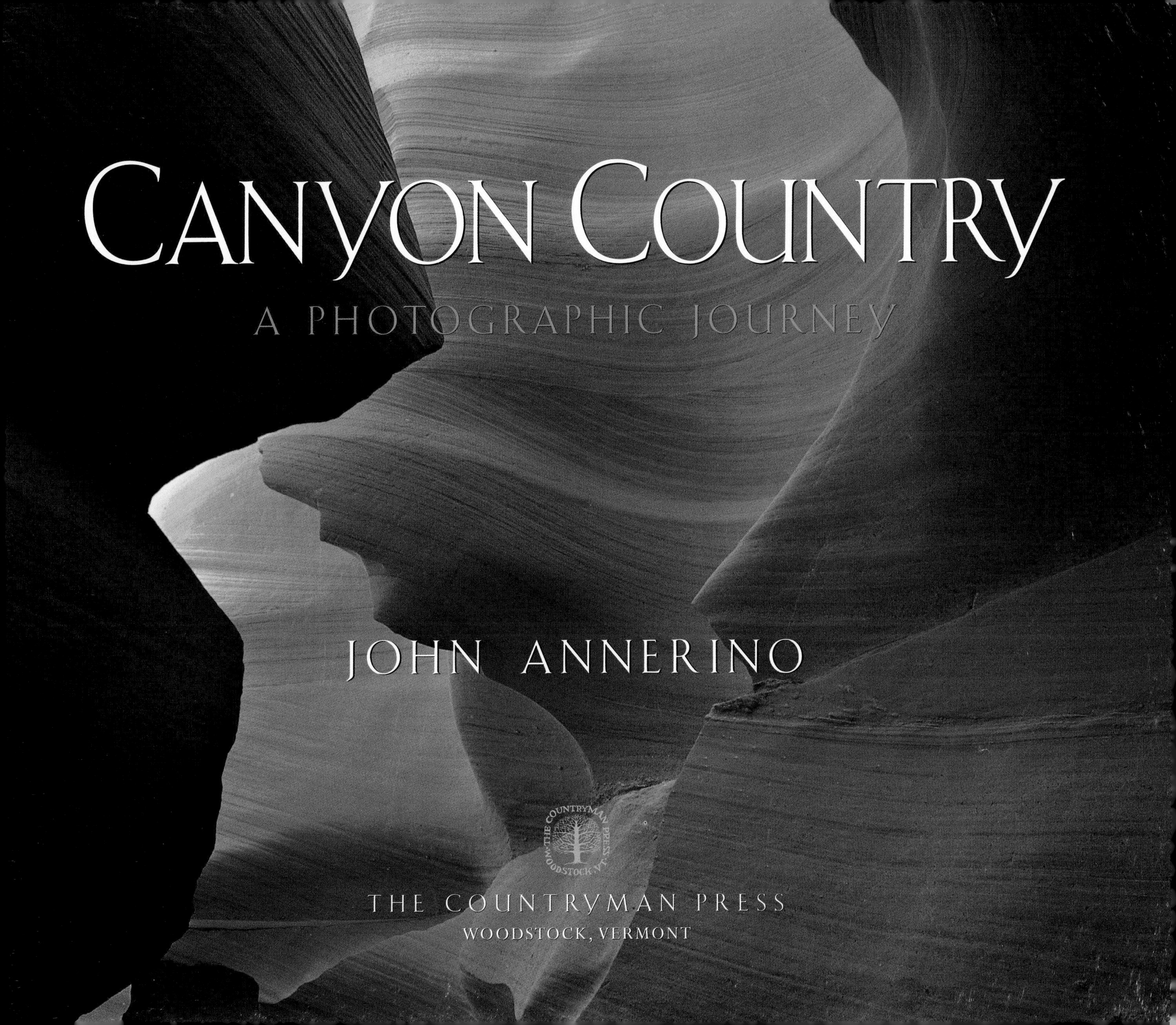

CANYON COUNTRY

A PHOTOGRAPHIC JOURNEY

JOHN ANNERINO

THE COUNTRYMAN PRESS
WOODSTOCK, VERMONT

Essays and photographs copyright © 2005 by John Annerino

First Edition

All rights reserved. No part of this book may be reproduced in any way by any electronic or mechanical means, including information storage and retrieval systems, without permission in writing from the publisher, except by a reviewer, who may quote brief passages.

ISBN 0-88150-661-3

Library of Congress Cataloging-in-Publication Data has been applied for.

Cover and interior design by Eugenie S. Delaney
Cartography by Jacques Chazaud

Published by The Countryman Press,
P.O. Box 748, Woodstock, Vermont 05091

Distributed by W. W. Norton & Company, Inc.,
500 Fifth Avenue, New York, NY 10110

Printed in Spain by Artes Graficas Toledo

10 9 8 7 6 5 4 3 2 1

PREVIOUS PAGE: *The Corkscrew, Lower Antelope Canyon, Arizona*

OPPOSITE PAGE: *Petrified sand, Coyote Buttes, Arizona*

Jefferson County Public Library, CO
1142675702

For Edward Abbey:
his pen first brought the slickrock to life,

Tad Nichols:
his camera was the last to see Glen Canyon before it was lost,

the singers, shamans, and medicine men:
their songs and visions still echo from the walls and stones.

"Whenever he went out by himself, he heard the songs of spirits sung to him . . . His three brothers had no faith in him. They said, 'When you have returned from your solitary walks & tell us you have seen strange things & heard strange songs, you are mistaken, you only imagine you hear these songs & you see nothing unusual.'"

—Washington Matthews, 1902
The Night Chant

ACKNOWLEDGMENTS

I'D LIKE TO THANK CRAIG SPILLMAN for opening the doors to scholarship—and Navajo Mountain—for me, Michael St. Clair for dragging my boat ashore in Cataract Canyon, Tom Thompson for inviting me to row the San Juan River, Tim Ganey for venturing down Hole in the Rock with me, Richard Nebeker who rarely said no to walking Paria Canyon, Hatch River Expeditions in Vernal, Utah, for hiring me to row the Green and Yampa rivers one summer, Steve Ward for piloting me across Lake Powell, and the Paiute and Navajo who opened their hearts to me during my journey. I want to thank my wife, Alejandrina, and young sons, John and Nathan, for enduring heat, cold, thunderstorms, tent fatigue, red ants, hungry ravens, mean squirrels, and burnt marshmallows. I'd also like to thank Lauren Blaurert and George Huey for their kind advice, Tony Ebarb and Theresa Ebarb for their generous counsel, and the University of Arizona Main, Science and Center for Creative Photography Libraries for their trove of research materials. If you are pleased with the book you're holding in your hands, by all means heap your praise on the talented people who helped bring it to this final stage: Deb Goodman, Eugenie S. Delaney, Richard Fumosa, Jennifer Thompson, Jacques Chazaud, David Corey, Kermit Hummel, and Bill Rusin. Lest we never forget, long before the rugged, wild, and beautiful country featured in this book became parklands, it was the ancestral homelands of the *Anaasází* (Navajo), *Mukwic* (Paiute and Ute), *Hisat'sinom* (Hopi), and other Pueblo peoples. Thank you.

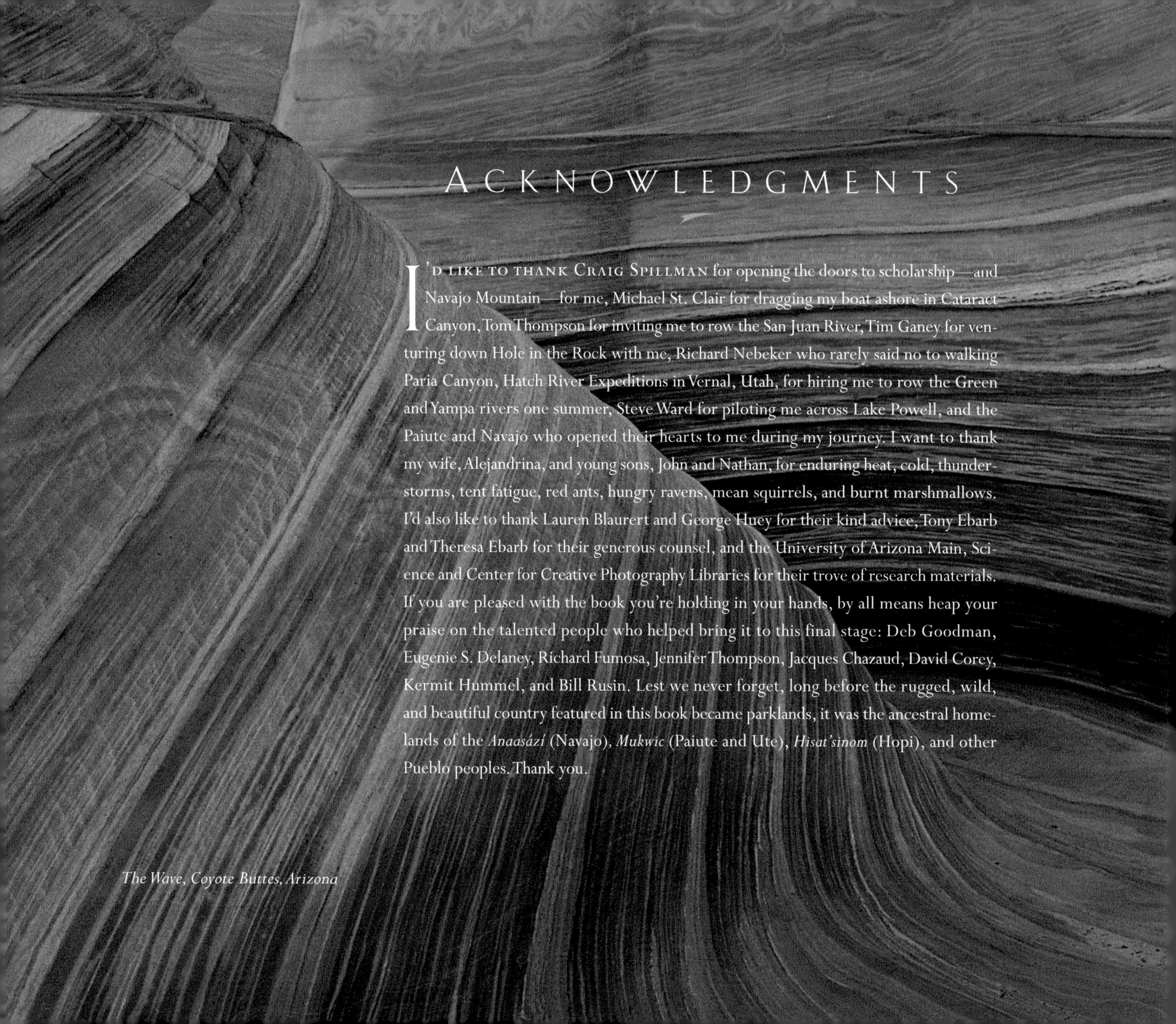

The Wave, Coyote Buttes, Arizona

CONTENTS

INTRODUCTION

"We have lived upon this land from the days beyond history's record,
far past any living memory, deep into the time of legend.
The story of my people and the story of this place are one single story.
No man can think of us without thinking of this place.
We are always joined together."

—PUEBLO ELDER, DATE UNKNOWN

A HOT WIND WHIPPED ACROSS THE PLATEAU, STINGING MY SKIN RAW with red sand. I covered my eyes and spit sand out of my teeth as I went about rigging my raft for a journey down the Colorado River. "The River," our bronze-skinned crew liked to call it. We were headed down the *Río Colorado* for a two-week voyage through the Grand Canyon when I first felt the irresistible pull of the canyon country upstream. Jagged peaks and sheer walls soared thousands of feet above our camp on the banks of the Colorado and Paria rivers, creating a sublime red mural that directed my gaze in one direction. I looked upriver into the mouth of Paria Canyon and wondered what lay beyond. A beautiful yet forbidding chasm in a far-flung corner of a forgotten world, non-Indians avoided it until John D. Lee had the gumption to drive a herd of cattle through its icy breach during the winter of 1871. A tough Mormon pioneer, polygamist, and fugitive from justice who was executed by a firing squad while he sat on his coffin, Lee established a ford in this wilderness of stone because it was the only place to cross the Colorado River for hundreds of miles in either direction.

By late afternoon the wind relented and my paddle boat was rigged, but I kept looking into the mysterious canyon, wondering what lay beyond. I needed to find out. It

Paria Canyon, Vermilion Cliffs, Arizona

PREVIOUS PAGE:
Marble Canyon Gorge, Grand Canyon, Arizona

would be another day before our passengers arrived and we launched a flotilla of small white boats down Marble Canyon—the first of many gorges that vanquished explorers trying to navigate a wild river through the uncharted depths of the Grand Canyon. So I took off at a trot and started running up Paria Canyon. Walls that had imprisoned Spanish padres Domínguez and Escalante in 1776 towered overhead, as I ran through a twisting labyrinth that lured me deeper into its embrace.

Night fell in the canyon, the air cooled, and a coyote moon climbed over the black rimrock. It was time to head back to camp, but I wanted to see what lay beyond the next turn in the moonlit chasm. I kept moving. This ancient travel corridor, first used by ancestral Pueblo peoples long before history's record, was the gateway to the Colorado Plateau. I'd spent years exploring the Grand Canyon, so I had a good sense of what awaited me below Lee's historic river crossing. But I didn't know what canyons, secrets, and discoveries awaited above. Author C. Gregory Crampton first pondered the Grand Canyon dilemma in his 1964 book, *Standing Up Country*: "Is this the only canyon? Are there others? What is the country upstream like? What men have passed through here?"

It took years to discover my own answers to those questions. Following river currents of explorers who ran the plateau's floodwaters in leaky wooden boats, tracks of pioneers' wagons that rolled across the slickrock on hand-forged steel rims, and canyon paths trod into the rimrock by the yucca-fiber sandals of ancestral *Anaasází* (Navajo), *Mukwic* (Paiute and Ute), and *Hisat'sinom* (Hopi), I embarked on many sojourns before I got a feel for the lay of the land and was touched by the spirits that were believed to inhabit it.

Paria Canyon opened the secret door to these mythic canyon lands, and my next journey into it marked me forever—a trek to Rainbow Bridge. Led by cowboy-explorer John Wetherhill and Paiute guides Nasja Begay and Jim Mike, archaeologist Dean Byron Cummings and government surveyor W. B. Douglass believed they were the first to make the long, arduous overland journey to Rainbow Bridge; they claimed "discovery" of the great natural wonder on August 14, 1909. First seen by Navajo medicine man Blind Salt

Lees Ferry, Glen Canyon, Arizona

Clansman in 1868 and later by gold miners in 1884, the joint Douglass and Cummings expeditions followed Paiute and Ute trails that were later used by Navajo refugees. I followed the same trails to Rainbow Bridge when I was asked to lead a group of Navajo students on a journey around Navajo Mountain. Their teachers said they were "troubled," but all they needed was time away from civilization.

Seen from distant points across the Colorado Plateau, from the Pink Cliffs in Utah to Kachina Peaks in Arizona, the blue dome of 10,388-foot Navajo Mountain is a sacred landmark for the *Diné* ("the people"). Navajo traditionalists call it *Naatsis'áán* ("Head of the Earth"), and it sits on the edge of ancestral homelands that span 30,000 square miles of the Four Corners region called *Dinetah* ("the land"). Under orders of Brigadier General James H. Carleton, Colonel Christopher "Kit" Carson waged a

Three Sisters,
Monument Valley,
Arizona

scorched-earth campaign against peaceful Navajo throughout *Dinetah* in 1863, and forced more than 9,000 people to embark on what became known as the Long Walk from Fort Defiance, Arizona, to Bosque Redondo, New Mexico. Hundreds perished of hunger and cold during the 300-mile march; pregnant mothers were shot on sight when they tried to escape; and others were kidnapped by New Mexican slave traders. But many fled the shackles of slave traders and muzzle blasts of Carson's troops. Upward of 2,000 Navajos sought refuge in the maze of canyons that gouged the rugged flanks of Navajo Mountain, from Rainbow Bridge to the desolate mesas rimming the San Juan and Colorado rivers.

Snake, Kachina Peaks summit, Arizona

I thought it would be good for seven young men to see the sacred refuge of their ancestors. Their elders agreed and blessed us before we left Tuba City, Arizona. In parting, they told us to say the Navajo prayer of Protection when we reached Rainbow Bridge.

Shouldering packs laden with ten days of rations and two days of water, we followed a rocky trail in and out of a half-dozen deep, slickrock canyons that drained Navajo Mountain before we plunged off the rimrock into Cliff Canyon. We threaded a gash in the canyon walls the next day and stopped for a break at Redbud Pass. In 1922, John Wetherhill guided a "tenderfoot and cliff-dweller from Manhattan" named Charles L. Bernheimer to Rainbow Bridge. But before Bernheimer could hail it as "one of the most inspiring marvels of the ages," Wetherhill and his men spent three days drilling and blasting a route for their pack train through Redbud Pass. When they were done prying away boulders with the stout limbs of redbud trees, they etched their names in the soft stone: *1922 Wetherhill Bernheimer*.

Using hand-carved toeholds that prospectors called "Moki steps," we climbed down the slickrock from Redbud Pass and reached Echo Springs after a day and a half in

the canyon heat. We dropped our packs at the foot of looming brown cliffs and took turns pressing our chapped lips to the mossy green seep. We drank our fill of the cool, sweet water, then followed sandy ledges along Bridge Creek until Rainbow Bridge came into view. When Wetherhill guided President Theodore Roosevelt and western writer Zane Grey to Rainbow Bridge in 1913, their adventure inspired Grey to write, "It was not for many eyes to see. The tourist, the leisurely traveler, the comfort-loving motorist would never behold it. Only by toil, sweat, endurance and pain could any man ever look at Non-nezoshe. It seemed well to realize that the great things of life had to be earned."

My charges had earned their right to see Rainbow Bridge. Declared a national monument by President William Howard Taft on May 30, 1910, Rainbow Bridge is the largest natural bridge in the world. Rivaling the height of the nation's Capitol, it's 290 feet tall and spans 275 feet. Awed by the sight of a tawny stone arcing across the turquoise sky from one canyon wall to the other, the young men recalled stories their elders had told them about *Na'nízhoozhí* ("Rainbow Rock-Span"). Until Lake Powell offered visitors motorized access to Rainbow Bridge, Navajo "singers" and medicine men made pilgrimages to the foot of the Rainbow to perform the Protectionway and Blessingway ceremonies. *Na'nízhoozhí* stood near the confluence of the San Juan and Colorado rivers, the "male and female rivers." The Cloud and Rain People were born from their sacred waters and were joined in mythic union at Rainbow Bridge.

In the years that unfolded, I heard the call of canyon country framed by this hallowed window of stone. This book is about those journeys, adventures, and scenes that were unveiled before my camera lens. I invite you to join me on trails that still lead deep into the time of legend, and to marvel at country that many eyes have still not seen.

OPPOSITE: *Echo Peaks, Navajo Indian Reservation, Arizona*

BELOW: *Navajo portrait, Rainbow Bridge, Utah*

ONE

CANYON COUNTRY

Nowhere But Here

"From one rim of the Grand Canyon,
you can easily see the opposite rim eight to ten miles away.
Standing on the edge of canyon country in Utah,
you would be one hundred miles away from the opposite side—
a hundred miles of canyons, mesas, buttes, reefs."
—C. Gregory Crampton, 1964
Standing Up Country

WE ARE STANDING ON THE EDGE OF CANYON COUNTRY IN UTAH. It has taken our party two hard days to reach the wind-wracked summit of Navajo Mountain from Rainbow Bridge. We are weary from the altitude and the grueling ascent, our feet are banged and blistered from the stones, and we are down to our last day of rations. We are headed down the other side of *Naatsis' áán*, an ancient laccolith that hovers 6,000 feet above the bloodred mesas of Navajoland. We plan to fill our half-empty canteens, heat a pot of day-old stew, and bivouac for the night at War God Spring. We will end our ten-day journey the next day, far below the sacred waters of Navajo deities *Naayéé' Neizghání* ("Monster Slayer") and *Tó Bá Jíshchíní* ("Born-for-Water"). But first we must stop to take in the view.

The cold wind whistles through a bent stand of limber pine. We huddle from its bite, protected by a black wall of volcanic rock. From our perch we can see "a hundred

Cliff Palace, Mesa Verde, Colorado

PREVIOUS PAGE: *Mitchell Mesa, Monument Valley, Arizona*

miles of canyons, mesas, buttes, [and] reefs." We are looking at the heartland of the Colorado Plateau. One of the last explored, least inhabited regions in the contiguous United States, the Colorado Plateau remains its most remote. Comprising 130,000 square miles of Arizona, Utah, Colorado, and New Mexico, the 6,000-foot Colorado Plateau is the second largest plateau on earth and forms one of the most rugged and astonishing landscapes in the world.

At our feet a sheer-walled inland sea stretches 180 miles from Dark Canyon in the northeast to Glen Canyon in the southwest. Called the "Jewel of the Colorado" by Floyd Dominy, "an independent cuss . . . and two-fisted drinker" from the Bureau of Reclamation, Dominy was the driving force behind an engineering marvel that choked the wild waters of the Colorado River behind Glen Canyon Dam. Escalante Creek, Crossing of the Fathers, Forbidding Canyon, Last Chance Creek, Coyote Gulch, more than one hundred tributary canyons, creeks, and gulches that breathed life into Glen Canyon were drowned by a lake named in honor of Major John Wesley Powell—the one-armed explorer who first navigated it in 1869.

As the sun plummeted through the orchid haze, and gold light gave way to blue, the future of my canyon journeys lay spread out before me on a sprawling map of fossilized sand. North of Glen Canyon I could see the Kaiparowits Plateau sweep fifty miles south across the copper-red landscape from the Table Cliffs to Dance Hall Rock. This rough, isolated, and inhospitable country—etched by a thousand different canyons—was the domain of the

Southern Paiute. They called it *Kaivavič* ("Mountain Lying Down"), and it was the center of their world. One summer, a friend and I drove hundreds of miles across the American outback and traced the backbone of the Kaiparowits Plateau to a breach in a canyon wall called Hole in the Rock. We scrambled down the steep, rugged notch to water's edge, taken by the pluck and fortitude of Mormon pioneers who chiseled and blasted a "hole in the rock" in order to lower eighty-three horse- and ox-driven wagons to a ferry waiting to take them across the Colorado River in the winter of 1879–80.

Studying the corrugated topography in the dwindling light, I peered down at the labyrinth of canyons that entwined the confluence of the Colorado and San Juan rivers. I traced the silver ribbon of the Colorado River through ramparts of terra-cotta mesas until it vanished from view in the mauve horizon; the future awaited me on its tributaries. I spent two months rowing the Green and Yampa rivers through Dinosaur National Monument when a friend invited me to raft the Colorado River through Canyonlands National Park. Confident I could run Cataract Canyon's "Big Drop Rapids" after a season of rowing Canyon of Lodore, Disaster Falls, and Whirlpool Canyon, my friend shared a thought with me around the campfire the night before we launched from our camp below Moab: "There are two kinds of boatmen: those who have flipped, and those who *will*." Drifting on silent currents through deep fissures and meanders toward Spanish Bottom, I didn't believe this, of course, until I got lost in a wave train of exploding brown haystacks in Rapid 23. A ten-foot V-wave of icy water

Wolf's Tooth, Capitol Reef, Utah

West Mitten Butte,
Monument Valley,
Arizona

broke over me, wrenching the wooden oars from my hands. The boat flipped, the lights went out, and I was dragged down to the bottom of the river. I breached for air, coughing up silt and snowmelt, and swam for my boat. But my cameras and film were gone, kept as a toll. The photographs I'd taken of Cataract Canyon were buried in sand, mud, and river cobble, not far from where Grand Canyon explorers Emery and Ellsworth Kolb pecked their names in the canyon walls during their run through Cataract Canyon in 1911.

Sacred Mountain,
San Francisco Peaks, Arizona

Darkness smothered the landscape, and flashlights stabbed the night sky. We crawled out of our summit lair, shouldered our packs, and walked stiff-legged down the muddy trail to War God Spring. I knew there would be other journeys into canyon country—though I didn't know what they would be, or that they would lead me through a landscape of desire I could not have imagined. I roamed among cloud-piercing spires, hairpin arches, vaulted mesas, and slickrock canyons that were found nowhere else in the world. Sculpted by howling winds, rushing water, and the ancient upheaval of great landmasses, it was the ancestral home of Native peoples who built precarious cliff dwellings that still stand a millennium later. The Colorado Plateau's landforms, life zones, and cultural history were so extraordinary among the earth's natural wonders, I saw firsthand the reason the entire region was nominated a World Heritage Site. Castellated mesas, burnt cliffs, eerie hoodoos, natural bridges, haunted canyons, and sacred mountains served as mileposts throughout my travels. They guided me from Glen Canyon to Zion Canyon, from Bryce Canyon to Capitol Reef, and from Canyonlands to Arches, then south over the brink of the Colorado Plateau back home.

Throughout the course of my journeys, Navajo Mountain was often in view. A black heart beating in red stone, it was a welcome presence in country cursed as Land's End. What struck me more, though, was the fact that many had called this hidden quarter of the Great Southwest "canyon country" in the first place. Seen from the serpentine chasms of the Green, San Juan, and Colorado rivers, or the dark narrows of Zion Canyon, Cliff Canyon, and Black Canyon of the Gunnison, it was a fitting description. But viewed from the rimrock of Island in the Sky, the mesas of Monument Valley, the breaks of Red Canyon, or the badlands of North Six-shooter Peak, I was surprised to discover, as Crampton wrote, "There is as much country standing up as there is laying down."

In a grand staircase that leads a hundred miles north from one rim of the Grand Canyon to the far rim of the Aquarius Plateau, my journeys through "standing up country" took me from Coyote Buttes to the White Cliffs, Paunsaugunt Plateau to the Waterpocket Fold, Dead Horse Point to the Book Cliffs, and much of the tortured and miraculous country in between. It was easy to see why few places in the West offered a better hideout for Butch Cassidy and the Sundance Kid's Wild Bunch. Why few locations offered a more dramatic backdrop for John Ford's movie classics *Stagecoach* and *The Greatest Story Ever Told*. And why few natural settings offered such soul-stirring inspiration for writers Zane Grey, Edward Abbey, and Tony Hillerman—and the trails of poets, artists, and photographers who preceded them.

Revered by Native peoples, probed by Spanish explorers, and traversed by government surveyors, it was a harsh, extraordinarily beautiful country that could not be denied. Gold seekers and uranium hunters went bust searching for its fabled riches—but the country would not let them go. Cowboys and sheepherders scratched out a toehold trying to graze stock on sage and blackbush—but the country would not let them go. Pioneers crossed the sand and slickrock trying to reach California—but the country would not let them go.

This was the country that held me in thrall. This was the country that marked my journeys. This was the country I had the privilege to see.

Canyon light,
Lower Antelope Canyon,
Arizona

RIGHT: *The Narrows, Zion, Utah*

OPPOSITE: *Thors Hammer, Bryce, Utah*

OPPOSITE: *Rainbow, Grand Staircase–Escalante, Utah*

LEFT: *Metate Arch, Grand Staircase–Escalante, Utah*

PREVIOUS PAGE:
Delicate Arch, Arches, Utah

RIGHT: *The Window, Lower Antelope Canyon, Arizona*

OPPOSITE: *Frijole Falls, Bandelier, New Mexico*

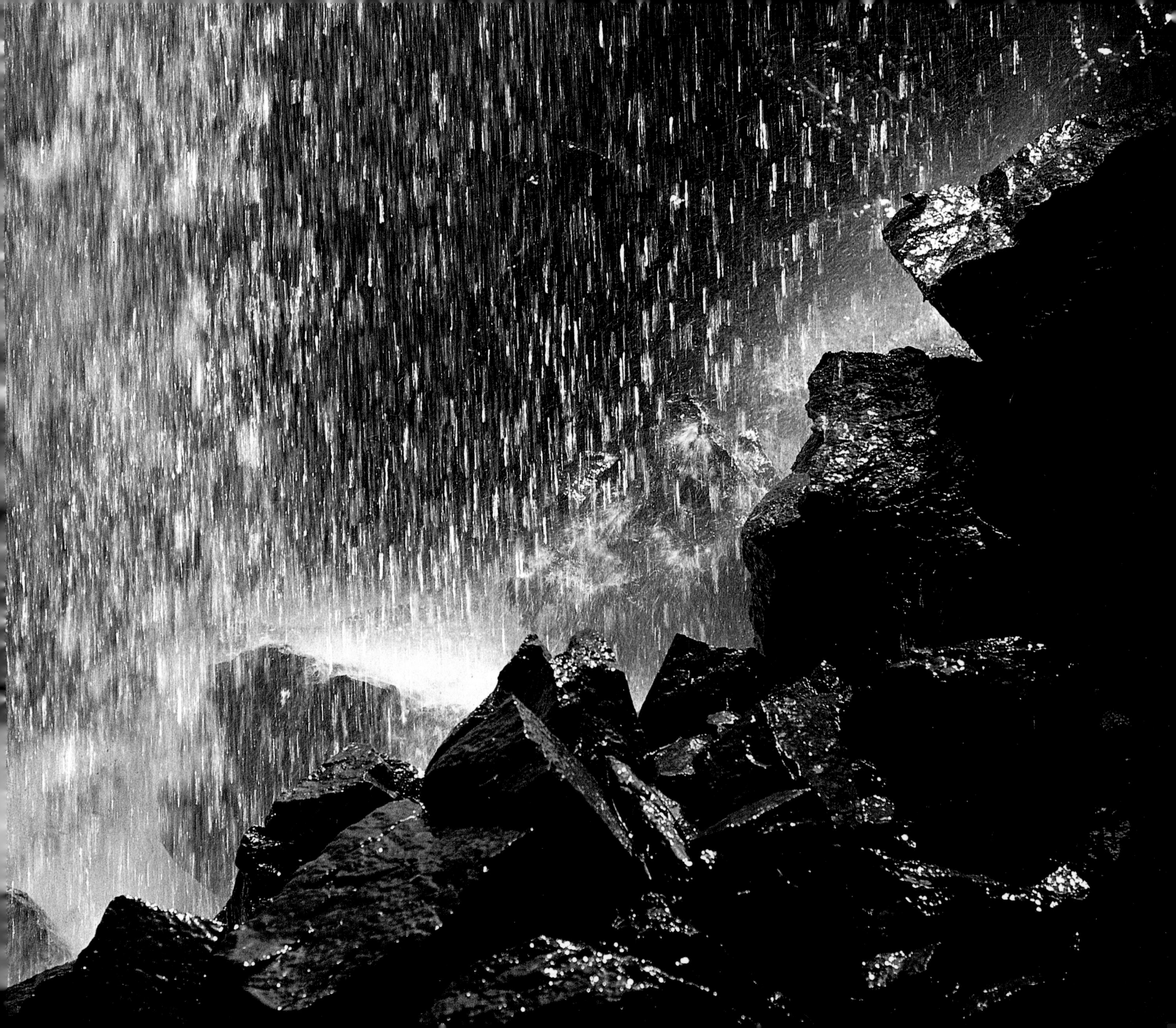

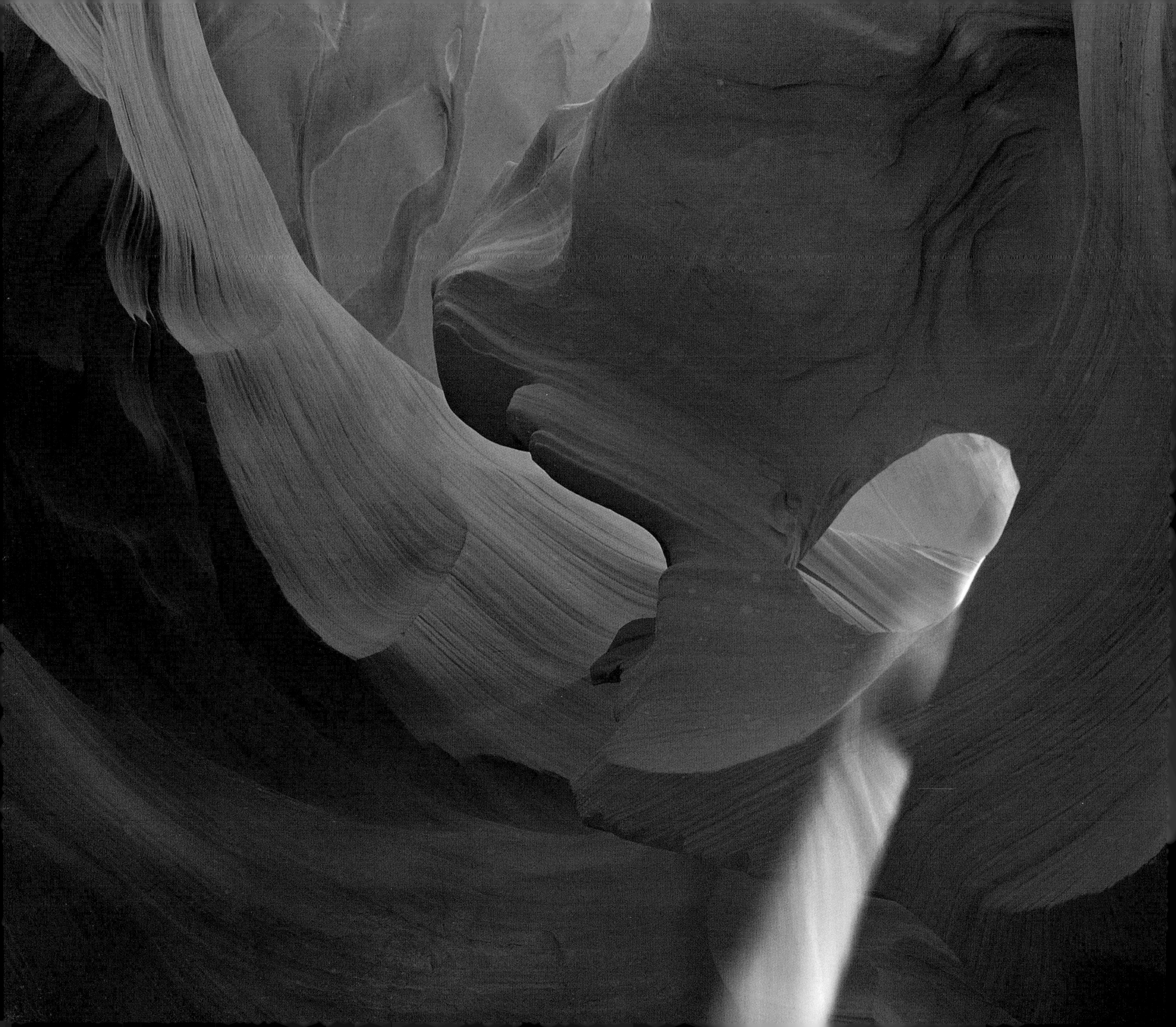

TWO

GRAND STAIRCASE, ESCALANTE, AND GLEN CANYON

The Place Where No One Lives

"I am exploring southward to the Colorado, where no one lives."
—Everett Ruess, 1934
On Desert Trails with Everett Ruess

WHERE NO ONE LIVES." I THOUGHT ABOUT THAT AS I SCURRIED across a catwalk of ledges into country I did not know. Black buzzards wheeled in the yellow sun, casting shadows the size of pterodactyls that swept back and forth across the Triassic stone. The August sun bore down on me as I followed crude stacks of brown rocks along a barren ridge. It led to slickrock etched with orthogonal patterns that resembled tortoise shells. I threaded a passage between twin cones of tepee-shaped rocks, and then made my way toward a tongue of sand that spilled down the cliff face a mile beyond. Two gallons of water sloshed in my pack as I leapt and danced off the rimrock to a lone tree that struggled for life at the foot of the sand. Except for the buzzards, I was alone. The only sounds I heard were my breathing and the whoosh of footsteps as I kicked my toes up a waterfall of sand toward a landscape that "seemed more beautiful to me than ever before."

Those were the words of a young wanderer and poet named Everett Ruess. He

PREVIOUS PAGE: *Eagles Eye, Lower Antelope Canyon, Arizona*

OPPOSITE: *Sunset, Wahweap Creek, Grand Staircase–Escalante*

crossed Grand Staircase, Escalante, and Glen Canyon country in 1934, and led his dog, Curly, and two burros from the last outpost of Escalante, Utah, down the Hole in the Rock Trail to Davis Gulch. That's where Ruess disappeared one cold November day. It might have been the twentieth or twenty-first. No one knows for certain. If they did, they went toes up before they could spill the secrets to a mystery that's gripped canyon country ever since. Some say Ruess vanished, swallowed by the immense landscape. Others believe he was murdered, his body sent down the Escalante River by sheepherders or "renegades." Still others reported sighting him in Old Mexico, living out new dreams. Whatever Ruess's fate, he left behind a trove of poems, diaries, letters, block prints, watercolors, and photographs that portrayed wanderlust for the place where no one lives. "The country between here and the San Juan and Colorado rivers and beyond them," Ruess wrote to his parents from camp on Navajo Mountain six months before search parties went looking for him, "is as rough and impenetrable a territory as I have ever seen."

Still is. The sun climbed higher as I kicked my way out of the sand and scrambled up cross-bedded sandstone toward a dark crack that looked like it would split the mountain in half. My T-shirt was drenched with sweat, and an adobe crust of mud, sand, and perspiration hung from my ankles and calves. I kept climbing until I reached shade. I took off my pack and felt the chill of hot air wick away the moisture. I sat down and peeled the cake off my legs. Gazing north, I traced my route across a spine of rock that cut the clear blue sky like a flint knife. In the distance, I could see dust stirring in the mirage of sand and stone. I took a long pull of water and watched the hot wind hurl a plume of sand hundreds of feet in the air; buzzards rode the thermal into the heavens until they disappeared. A dust devil started to build, twisting this way and that through piñon and juniper, around pyramids of rosette stone, across the sand and sagebrush badlands.

I was sitting in a trough of petrified sand, walled in on three sides, when the *remolino* spun up the sand spit. I crouched down, covered my eyes with a bandana, and

sheltered my camera bag with grit-covered hands and sun-baked arms. Hot wind slammed against the wave of rock. I crouched lower, trying to melt into the landscape before the brunt of the storm hit, but there was no escaping it. Furnace wind engulfed me, lashing me with a dervish of burning sand that howled around me, plugging my ears and nose.

It was the middle of summer. I was probing the edges of Grand Staircase–Escalante National Monument when the sandstorm hit. A big, bad, beautiful country, I'd read it beckoned and defied all comers. There was no disputing that. Created in 1996 by President Bill Clinton under the century-old Antiquities Act, the 1.7-million-acre monument rivals the size of Delaware, Rhode Island, and Washington, D.C., combined. Together with Escalante Canyon, Glen Canyon, and the mystifying network of canyons that link them, it forms a daunting landscape to explore by foot, saddle, or pickup. When Herbert E. Gregory surveyed the 5,400-square-mile Kaiparowits country on a pack mule for the U.S. Geological Survey in 1915, he wrote, "The region is desolate and abandoned even by the Indians; it is a 'no man's land' that separates the Utes from the roving Navajos."

Journey into this region today and you do so at your own risk. You are off the grid. Paved roads do not exist. Dirt roads turn into rivers of mud. You cannot phone for help. Make a mistake here, and if you can't get out under your own power, chances are you will walk off the face of the earth. Just the sort of country that tugs at your soul. A palette of sandstone escarpments mortared together by badlands of shale and siltstone, the western third of this no-man's-land is called the Grand Staircase; it climbs

Grosvenor Arch,
Grand Staircase–Escalante

thousands of feet up from the high desert of the Vermilion Cliffs, Chocolate Cliffs, White Cliffs, and Grey Hills to the Pink Cliffs and ancient forest of the Paunsaugunt Plateau, exposing an iris of stones, fossils, and seabeds that date back 200 million years.

Its central core is the Kaiparowits Plateau; a lofty, yet arid land the Paiutes called *Kaivavič* ("Mountain Lying Down"), it is cut off from the outside world by the hundred-mile-long, serrated teeth of the Cockscomb to the west, the deep, dead sea of Glen Canyon to the south, and the Straight Cliffs of Fiftymile Bench to the east.

Its eastern third is known as Escalante Canyons; draining 2,000 square miles, the Escalante River Basin was not mapped until Powell surveyor Almon Harris Thompson laid eyes on it in 1872 and wrote: "A large portion of this area is naked sandstone rock, traversed in all directions by a perfect labyrinth of narrow gorges."

A week after I emerged from the sandstorm at Coyote Buttes, I wandered among the hoodoos of Devils Garden seventy raven miles north. A bank of gray clouds rolled over the Straight Cliffs that hugged the Kaiparowits Plateau. "Fiftymile Mountain" was the term pioneers headed down the Hole in the Rock Trail liked to use. Thunder boomed in the distance, as I stood near the base of a delicate arch that was said to look like a stone Native people used for grinding seeds. The light was dismal, sleet gray—perfect for black-and-white film. So I stowed my gear and started poking around the nooks and crannies of sandstone goblins that looked more like something out of a Lewis Carroll fantasy than anything menacing or evil.

Lightning struck yards away, igniting a flash of blue light and thunder that took my breath away. The earth shook, and the air grew cold as thunder and lightning struck the megaliths like cannon fire. Smoky clouds rolled in and sheets of hail pelted the ground, covering the red sand with a crystal-white veneer that looked like rock salt. Scorched by hot wind and sand the week before, I huddled over my camera bag shivering in a T-shirt, as a gush of brown water cascaded down a flute of stone nearby. The summer monsoons had arrived.

I was planning to follow Everett Ruess's trail through Davis Gulch. A few years previously, I'd traced the route of pioneers down Hole in the Rock. Now I wanted to see where Ruess "vanished—into thin air." I wanted to walk out the possibilities, but monsoons would turn the fifty-mile-long Hole in the Rock road into a quagmire. Days earlier I'd spoken with a ranger while driving the dusty washboard track between Kodachrome Basin and Grosvenor Arch. He told me about three Germans who ignored storm warnings and drove their rental car down Cottonwood Canyon. The slick mud and clay buried their vehicle up to its axles. The only reason they made it out alive, he said, was that the driver walked thirty miles out to the highway for help. But the other two remained stranded for four days without food until the road dried out and rangers could reach them.

Lightning drilled the landscape, and thunder shook the heavens. I could do nothing now but wait for the storm to break—and hope the huge stones didn't topple over me. I sat, shivered, and watched a torrent of brown water flash down the arroyo that stood between me and my truck. Twisting through rain-slick hoodoos, the water poured off the rim into Right Hand Collet Canyon and emptied into Twenty Mile Wash. Follow the Escalante River far enough below Twenty Mile Wash, say, ten days, and you'll reach Ruess's campsite in Davis Gulch. Ruess wrote, "Sunset made all the misery worth enduring. Far to the north and east stretched the purple mesas, with cloudbanks everywhere above them. Some were golden brown and vermilion where sunshafts pierced the low clouds. A rainbow glowed for a moment in the south. That was a promise." I looked out from the dark, damp overhang and saw that was my promise, too.

OPPOSITE: *Twilight, Kodachrome Basin*

OPPOSITE: *Sunbeams, Lower Antelope Canyon, Arizona*

LEFT: *Eagles flight, Upper Antelope Canyon, Arizona*

RIGHT: *Towers of Silence, Jack Riggs Flat, Grand Staircase–Escalante*

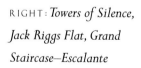

OPPOSITE: *The Goblins, Devils Garden, Grand Staircase–Escalante*

OPPOSITE: *Hoodoos, the Rimrocks, Grand Staircase–Escalante*

LEFT: *Monolith, Kodachrome Basin*

Sand pipe, Kodachrome Basin

Goblins, Devils Garden,
Grand Staircase–Escalante

THREE

ZION CANYON

If Walls Could Talk

"In some places the holes are so deep that we have to swim, and our little bundles of blankets and rations are fixed to a raft of driftwood . . . we cross and recross the stream, and wade along the channel where the water is so swift as to almost carry us off our feet . . . we are in danger every moment of being swept down, until night comes."

—J. W. Powell, 1870

Exploration of the Colorado River of the West

I followed the dark river upstream toward a beam of amber light that fell thousands of feet into the chasm. Cold water rushed over my knees, chilling my bones whenever I stopped moving, slowly filling my shoes with sand. Wherever I went in canyon country, there was no escaping the sand. This journey was no different. It formed the sheer walls that soared so high above me they pinched out the daylight. It formed the house-sized boulders that fell from craggy rims, forcing me to wade through deep holes that lapped at my pack. It formed the moss-covered stones I slipped and slid on whenever I pushed too hard against the current. Carried by the ancient river, it ground its way through a canyon shrouded in myth, legend, and darkness.

I crossed and recrossed a stream the Paiute called *Mukun'tuweap* ("Straight Canyon Stream"), wondering what words passed from their lips. I waded through a canyon they named *I-u-goone* ("Like an Arrow Quiver"), wondering why they believed there was only one way into and one way out of their hidden passage. I ran my fingers and palms across the soft texture of the canyon's elegant walls, wondering what drove out the Paiute from the canyon before nightfall. For the Parrusits band of Southern Paiute, *I-u-goone* was a place of reverence and fear. The friendly Wolf-god, *Shinna'wav*, stood near its entrance; the evil spirit *Wai-no-pits* inhabited its dark shadows.

In keeping with Paiute beliefs, Major John Wesley Powell also called the canyon *Mukun'tuweap* when he first explored it on September 12, 1870. In order to reach the foot of it, Powell and his men struggled for two days descending the neighboring *Pa-rú-nu-weap* ("Roaring Water Canyon"). On September 11, Powell wrote, "Wading again this morning; sinking in the quicksand, swimming the deep waters, and making slow and painful progress where the waters are swift, and the bed of the stream rocky." They had been following the East Fork of the Virgin River, and the day after they emerged from its grip they traveled north from the Mormon hamlet of Shunesburg, Utah, through a beautiful valley some locals called Not Zion. Brigham Young had visited the settlement that year and told his followers, "it was not Zion." *Not* fell out of use and Zion Canyon was given to the North Fork of the Virgin River canyon Powell explored.

That's where I was headed, through Zion Narrows toward shafts of sunlight that lit up the canyon walls like candle lanterns. I'd walked the North Fork of the Virgin River before, tracing its course from the lofty forests of the 8,500-foot-high Kolob Terrace. I slithered under logjams and climbed down chock stones as the river wound its way past Deep Creek, Kolob Creek, Goose Creek, and Orderville Canyon. I waded through chest-deep water—carrying my pack over my head, and I drank from plumes of water that cascaded hundreds of feet down the cliffs into

PREVIOUS PAGE:
Court of the Patriarchs

BELOW: *Cairn, The Narrows*

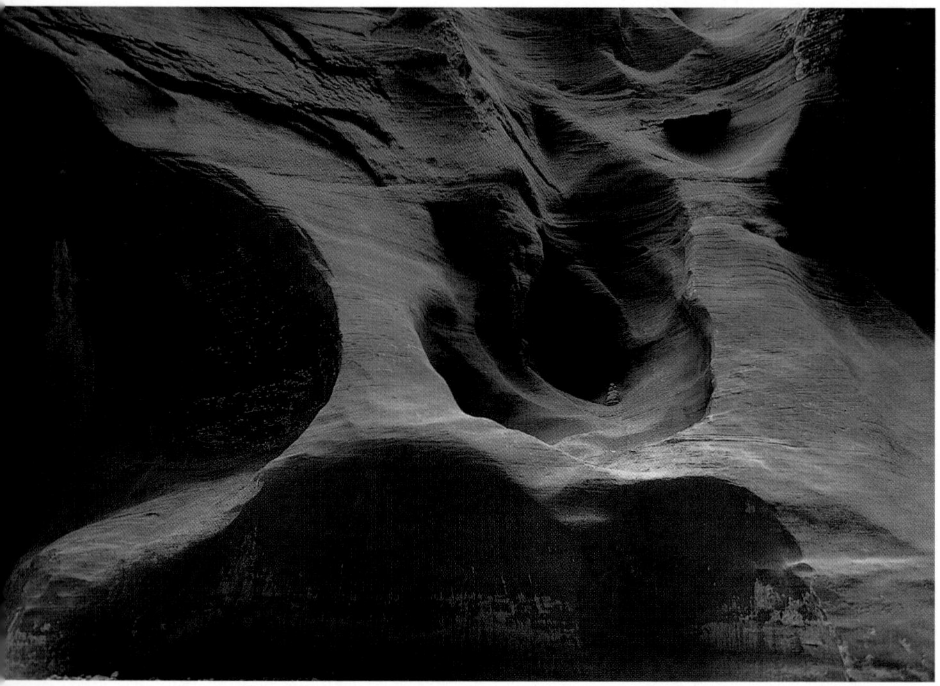

Box elder, The Narrows

my metal coffee cup. When I finally reached the pulpit rock of *Shinna'wav* at the mouth of the Zion Canyon, I had followed the length of a tiny river that carved a sixteen-mile-long, 2,000-foot-deep gorge through Jurassic sandstone. But I never really saw the canyon from the crowds. I'd walked it with eight companions, and, more often than not, we were overrun by lines of other parties wading up- and downstream.

On this day I decided to walk The Narrows alone. I started out in the early afternoon, but hundreds of men, women, and children had already piled out of shuttle buses minutes and hours ahead of me. In my hurry to pass the throngs, I slipped on the mossy stones, catching myself before I fell in the knee-deep water. But I didn't see a thing for miles, except people, water, and rock. So I climbed onto a sandy floodplain, sat down, leaned against the wall, and just waited.

When the last glimmer of sunlight flickered out of the canyon, I watched parades of hikers flee down the canyon as darkness crept in. I waded back into the middle of the stream, and for the first time that day I noticed seeps of water pouring out of the canyon walls. Rain and snowmelt that trickled hundreds of feet down honeycombs of Navajo Sandstone can take up to 1,200 years to reach the "spring line," where the ancient water wept from the walls.

I walked down the canyon alone, relishing the solitude and the music of running water, but I couldn't take my eyes off the watercolors that bled from the canyon walls. They reminded me of pictographs I'd seen in Sego Canyon, far to the north in the Book Cliffs. Archaeologists called them "anthropomorphs" and speculated that they represented shamans painted with natural dyes and pigments by Archaic hunters and gatherers during the Barrier Canyon period 3,000 to 4,000 years ago. These figures were different, painted by nature not by hand. Everywhere I looked life-sized figures stared down from the canyon walls. They were cloaked in black robes trimmed in silver, and they fell from their heads to their feet. They resembled R. C. Gorman paintings. There were hundreds of them, grouped in families, ceremonies, encampments, and villages, and

OPPOSITE: *Weeping walls, The Narrows*

Angels Landing

they blossomed from hanging gardens that festooned the walls above the river.

Were these the Spirit Seeps people sometimes talked of? Were they descendants of *Wai-no-pits* who drove the Par-rusits out of *I-u-goone* before nightfall? Were they the tears of slain Paiute crying from the walls of The Narrows? Or were they the rebirth of the *nɨmɨncimɨ* ("people"), prophesied by Wovoka, a Northern Paiute shaman who envisioned the Ghost Dance on his death bed during the solar eclipse of January 1, 1889: "When the sun died, I went up to heaven and saw God and all the people who had died a long time ago."

If walls could talk, I might know. I felt something palpable, it was benevolent, and it moved me. There was no explaining it, nor expecting anyone to believe me. I was alone, and I felt eyes follow me down the river as I strode out of the dark canyon into the daylight.

I boarded a shuttle and watched the setting sun paint the ramparts of Zion Canyon gold, pink, then purple as we headed down canyon toward the campground. I felt like a little boy. I was giddy. Something had touched me in Zion Narrows.

I woke before daybreak the next morning and huddled at the foot of the Temples of the Virgin waiting for the sun to rise. I was alone. The air was cold. And a dark wind blew out from the mouth of Zion Canyon. On cue, chickadees, flycatchers, and doves began singing as the first hint of sun painted the crests of the temples purple. As the sun rose higher, a cascade of colors tinted the walls pink, gold, yellow, then ivory. Poet-geologist Clarence E. Dutton viewed the scene during the Powell survey, and described it in his 1882 *Tertiary History of the Grand Cañon:* "In an instant there flashed before us a scene never to be forgotten . . . the most exquisite of its kind which the world discloses. The scene before us was the Temples and Towers of the Virgin." Dutton got it right, and it was the kind of prose that brought notice to Zion Canyon. On July 31, 1909, President William Howard Taft established Mukuntuweap National Monument, but the name didn't stick. A decade later, it became Zion National Park.

That afternoon, I climbed up to Angels Landing, an anvil of rock that towered 1,500 feet above the floor of Zion Canyon. I wanted a raptor's view of country that still claims to have the tallest sandstone cliffs in the world. From my perch, the northwest face of the 6,744-foot-high Great White Throne formed an imposing 2,200-foot-high wall that looked like a "brick standing on end" to Yosemite climbers Galen Rowell, Fred Beckey, and Pat Callis; their party made Zion's first big wall ascent when they scaled it in 1967. Behind the Great White Throne stood Cable Mountain. In 1906, writer Angus Woodbury rode horseback through the night over perilous trails that led from the East Rim to the floor of Zion Canyon. Riding around a dead packhorse that had fallen down the mountain earlier, Woodbury wrote, "The full moon was shining into the depths of the canyon . . . [I] slept out the night in . . . saddle blankets under the enchanting witchery of the starry heavens between the brilliant walls that seemed to reach the sky."

I sat on the edge of the cliff until nightfall, mesmerized by the play of shadow and light off walls the color of sun-bleached bones. It was a perfect aerie for a bivouac, but it was time to go. Stars lit up the night. I stood up, traversed a ridgeline that reached the sky, then floated down the mountain dreaming of Zion Narrows. It had touched the souls of Native peoples. It had touched the souls of explorers. And, I'd discovered, it had touched the souls of modern pilgrims.

The Great White Throne

East Temple

Hikers, Zion Narrows

RIGHT:

The Palisades,
East Temple

OPPOSITE:

Towers of the Virgin

The Narrows

Treetops and red rock,
Virgin River Narrows

Spires, Bridge Mountain

Virgin River Narrows

FOUR

CAPITOL REEF

Land's End

"No place left to hide. Violent death had thinned the ranks . . .
of the Wild Bunch. Butch Cassidy now could read very clearly the hand
writing on the wall . . . it was just a matter of time . . . barbed wire was
everywhere . . . once friendly ranchers were closing their doors."

—James D. Horan, 1949

Desperate Men

I squinted my eyes. It was high noon. A blinding white sun beat down on me. Hot sand burned the soles of my feet. And a river of sweat ran down my back. Hoofbeats thundered through the canyons, voices echoed off the walls. Gunfire ricocheted from the rimrock, blood spattered in the sand. I heard the creak of saddle leather, the snorting of horses on the run. I saw lather dripping from their bridles, flying horseshoes raking up rooster tails of sand. Galloping stirrup-to-stirrup, I watched a band of outlaws ride by as the canyon walls closed in. I was walking into the past.

I walked down the narrow gorge into a box canyon, wondering what it was like to drive a remuda of stolen horses through the fortress of stone. I made a dogleg turn to the south, then another to the north, wondering what it was like to haul saddlebags bursting with payrolls of $20 gold pieces beneath cliffs that hollered *ambush*. I followed a dry arroyo that twisted like a sidewinder, wondering what it was like to ride hell-for-leather one step ahead of a posse of lawmen, bounty hunters, and Pinkerton detectives hot on your tail.

Solution pockets, Capitol Gorge

PREVIOUS PAGE: *Wolf's Tooth*

I was on the trail of Robert Leroy Parker and Harry Longabaugh. They called themselves Butch Cassidy and the Sundance Kid. At one time or another, their roster of two-legged varmints included "Kid Curry" (Harry Logan), "Tall Texan" (Ben Kilpatrick), "Flat Nose" (George Currie), and Etta Place, the one woman and only member who fessed up to a real name—and "she could ride like a Sioux wind," to boot. Constables and sheriffs who tacked up the wanted posters called them the Wild Bunch. They rode into the sunset, but there was no place left to hide. In death—or in Bolivia—they became legends too tough to die.

I was tracking their canyon passage through a jungle of rock called Waterpocket Fold. Stretching across an ocean of desert a hundred miles from north to south, the rugged reef climbed 7,355 feet into navy-blue skies. During an uplift of the Colorado Plateau sixty million years ago, the earth's skin wrinkled, forcing one sedimentary rock layer over the other, producing a nearly impenetrable barrier that divided southern Utah in half. Few trails crossed the ancient upheaval of sandstone, siltstone, mudstone, shale, clay, volcanic ash, fossils, and petrified wood that created a hellish terrain of cliffs, canyons, breaks, and domes. The trails that did were rugged. They were hard to find. They rumbled with rockfall. And they snaked through a dead man's noose of canyons that God forgot. There was Fremont River Gorge; some 10,000 years ago, nomadic hunters and gatherers used it to cross the north end of the great barrier. There was Muley Twist Canyon; during the 1880s, ferryman Charles Thaddeus Hall followed a gorge through the south end of the Fold that was so narrow mules had to "twist" to get through it. There was Grand Wash; when dime novelists were writing the closing chapters of the Old West, cattlemen used it to cross the Fold between summer and winter pastures. And there was Capitol Gorge; during the 1890s, the Wild Bunch used it to ride from Robbers Roost in the San Rafael Swell to Butch's birthplace in Circle Valley, where he sometimes hung his holsters and hat. In time, Capitol Gorge became the gateway to the "Outlaw Empire," in an era of bank robbers, train bandits, cattle rustlers, horse thieves, and congenial desperados some townsfolk, ranchers, and kin had taken a liking to.

The voices, hoofbeats, and gunfire had fallen silent. The trail had gone cold. I followed the sandy, boulder-strewn wash beneath castellated walls of Wingate Sandstone. Monsoon rains and flash floods had been forecasted for late afternoon, forcing me to walk in the Dutch oven heat if I wanted to see the outlaw trail. The Southern Paiute had a simple but telling name for the Waterpocket Fold—they called it *Tɨmpiavič* ("Rock Mountain"). Together with the Circle Cliffs they called *Kaɨyɨgacɨ* ("Mountain Turn"), it was a forbidding barrier that was seldom crossed. It was land's end for the Paiute who lived to the west, and the place they did not go for the Ute who lived to the east.

Pioneer register, Capitol Gorge

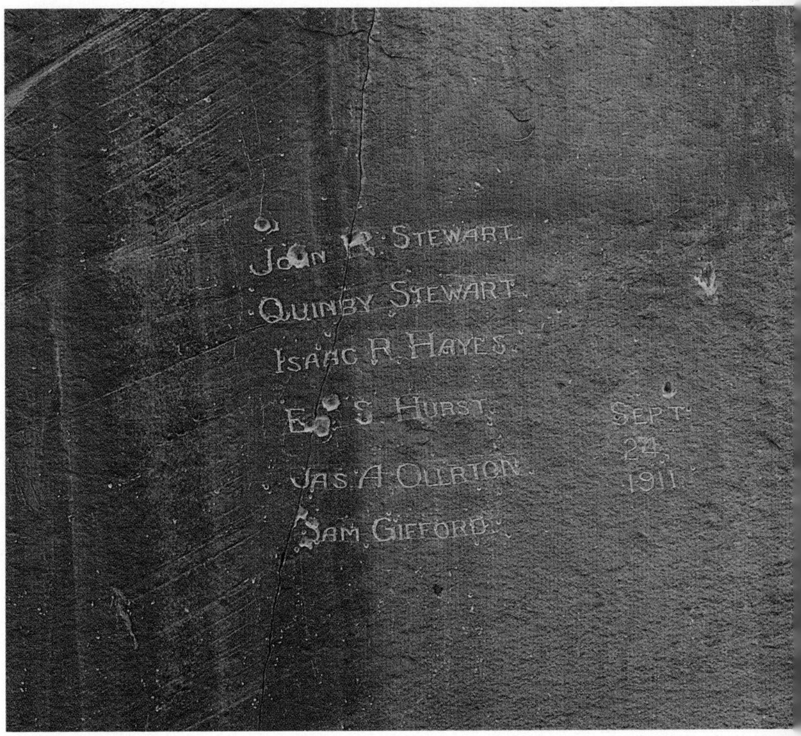

High on the south wall I saw a strange petroglyph. I stopped. It was not the handiwork of ancestral *Mukwic* (Paiute and Ute), or the Desert Culture, who carved figures of horned men in the Fremont River Gorge. It was a "pioneer register," chiseled by prospectors, settlers, or pioneers. How they climbed so high up the sheer cliff puzzled me. It was beyond the reach of a man standing on a saddle in boots and spurs or, for that matter, on a water barrel lashed to a buckboard. I didn't recognize the names pecked into the bullet-riddled stone:

John R. Stewart
Quinby Stewart
Isaac R. Hayes
E. S. Hurst
Jas A. Ourton
Sam Gifford
Sept. 24, 1911

The soft hoofbeats of deer eating peaches and the muffled roar of the Fremont River woke me the next morning. I brewed a pot of coffee as

sunlight danced through the treetops of the historic Mormon homestead. I finished my coffee and drove a narrow, winding road beneath a wall of brown cliffs to the head of Grand Wash. I stopped near the mouth of a canyon that cut in from the south. I got out of the truck and walked in the cool morning shade toward a pillar of stone that had turned my head at sundown the day before. I scrambled up heaps of knife-edged boulders that had fallen at its feet, careful not to start a slide. I bushwhacked through brambles of what looked like turbinella oak, careful not to rake my hands and arms with thorn-tipped leaves. When I reached the base of the stone, a prism of sunlight had climbed over the rim of the canyon. The canyon was called *Shinob*, after "the second great god of the Paiutes." He was the younger brother of *Tobats* who created the world. "Shinob," William R. Palmer wrote, "looked over the world that Tobats had made and said, 'It is good. It is strong. It is pretty.' Standing at the foot of an imposing monument that towered a hundred feet or more above, it looked like a Navajo woman weaving on a loom of cliffs. It was pretty, but it was hot.

I slithered down the rockslide, and walked along a creek bed of dry gravel that burned my face with the glaring heat. In most parts, creeks and rivers earn their names when they're running with water. In the dammed-up, damned-if-you-do/damned-if-you-don't, contrary landscape of the West, they're often called creeks and rivers when they're dry as boot leather, and cursed as floods when they slake the thirst of drought-stricken cattle. My lips were cracked, and my mouth was parched. I pulled a jug of ice water from my pack and hoisted it to my lips. The cold water cooled my throat. I doused my bandana and watched the salt run into the sand. I wiped my face and neck. I could think clearly again.

That afternoon, I visited Fremont River Gorge. I sat down on the banks of a stream that would, in time, become the elusive Dirty Devil River that Powell's men finally discovered. I lay back in the shade and watched clouds spin through a narrow window of cliffs. I listened to the peaceful melody of running water, as riffles soothed

OPPOSITE: *Evil Rock*

Navajo Dome, Waterpocket Fold

OPPOSITE: *Hickman Bridge, Fremont River Gorge*

my feet. But I had to leave. I laced on my shoes, shouldered my pack, and climbed up the rimrock. The rock was white, the trail was hot and steep, but the sky was blue. I was headed to Hickman Bridge, named for Joseph S. Hickman who led an effort during the 1920s to protect the Waterpocket Fold. I sat down in the shade when I reached the bridge and looked up. The truss of Kayenta Sandstone spanned 133 feet and stood 125 feet above the gorge. Hickman's efforts had paid off. President Franklin D. Roosevelt established Capitol Reef National Monument on August 2, 1937; it became a national park in 1971.

I walked back down the trail into the late-afternoon sun. It was starting to show some mercy—and color. High above the river on the south rim of Fremont River Gorge, a sharp fang poked out of the rimrock. There was no name for it on my map, so I called it Wolf's Tooth. Waves of white sand and an ocean of blue sky surrounded it as far into the horizon as I could see. *Shinob* had said the world *Tobats* created for the Paiute was good, it was strong, and it was pretty. *Shinob* had also said, "It is useless." And that was good to see, a wild, beautiful piece of country that had been pretty much left alone, as it had been set down in legends of long ago. Here at Land's End, in the Waterpocket Fold. And it still looked like a pretty good place to hide, too.

RIGHT: *Shinob, Shinob Canyon*

OPPOSITE: *Juniper skeleton, Capitol Gorge*

Rocky Mountain juniper,
Slickrock Divide

Grand Wash Narrows

Castellated walls, Capitol Gorge

OPPOSITE: *Twilight, The Castle*

Solution pockets, Fremont River Gorge

OPPOSITE: *Twilight, Chimney Rock*

The Great Curtain, Slickrock Divide

OPPOSITE: *Daybreak, Wildcat Mesa*

FIVE

BRYCE CANYON

Way Over *That* Way

"It's a hell of a place to lose a cow."
—Ebenezer Bryce, 1875

STARS FLICKERED LIKE DIAMONDS IN HEAVENS OF BLACK VELOUR. It was o'-dark-thirty. And the sun wouldn't show its colors for another hour. I walked along the edge of the Paunsaugunt Plateau, searching for traces of the Paria River. I'd followed the bloodlines of the river before. Paiutes called it the *Paria-pa* ("Elk Water"), and it ran through deep veins of sinuous red rock all the way to the river they called *Paga* ("Big Water"). It was a four-day journey from the head of the canyon to the Colorado River. I'd made it off and on throughout the years because I was drawn to the solace and beauty the rivers had made. Even then, I'd known the Paria River roared with flash floods fed by storm water that roared through the breaks beneath my feet, but I had never been to its source. That's what I was searching for now, origins that would lead to a lost river I hoped would reveal itself in the horizon.

I followed the path off the rim into a sea of darkness. Paiute called the woodlands at my back *Paunsagantɨ* ("Beaver Place"). That's what they said it looked like. The Paunsaugunt Plateau reared up out of the landscape between the Sevier River on the west and the Paria River on the east, stopping short of Skutumpah Terrace above the White Cliffs on the south. Eight thousand three hundred sixteen feet high, it was covered with forests of piñon and juniper, yellow pine, spruce, and aspen.

Totems, the Fairyland

PREVIOUS PAGE: *Hoodoos, the Fairyland*

The trail fell beneath this world, and I followed it through tall shadows, the soles of my shoes crunching on small brittle stones. The air was crisp, still, and quiet until I heard rustling in the dry leaves. It was loud. The hair on my neck stood up. I stopped and stared into the inky blackness, trying to make out a shape, and hoping I wouldn't see a pair of yellow eyes staring out from the darkness. I couldn't tell if it had claws and teeth, or feathers and a beak. Whatever it was, it then vanished. I took a deep breath and continued down the path, feeling my way with the soles of my feet.

I stopped in the silence when I saw first light blink through the hollow eyes of a black stone. It was the size of a juniper tree, and it looked like the ceremonial mask of an Apache *Ga'an* ("Mountain Spirit"). I stood up on my toes and peered through one eye at the horizon. A ribbon of yellow light winked through a crevice of charcoal clouds and the purple rim of the Kaiparowits Plateau. Paiutes had crossed that sagebrush sea on foot; they called it "the land," and they clawed at its mesas, cliffs, and canyons for a meager diet of lizards, piñon nuts, and, when hunting was good, deer or desert bighorns. Surveyors had crossed the same country on horseback; they called it a "territory," and they filled in the blank spots on their maps, tallying up resources of water, timber, minerals, and farmland that might offer an outside chance to settlers tough enough to wrest a living on the far side of civilization. Pioneers had crossed the same country in wagons; they called it a "frontier," and they looked high and low for a place to put down stakes, cordon off pastures with rip-gut fences, praise the Lord, and work from sunup to sunset on a place they could call their own. But no one, so far as is known, not even Major Powell or his point men like Thompson or Dutton, had traced the course of the Paria River, from the Colorado River, to its headwaters in the Pink Cliffs. "As one old-timer expressed it," Herbert E. Gregory wrote, "they were far from home, looking for Indians, not scenery; big cliffs and canyons are everywhere in Utah."

But nothing was quite like the Pink Cliffs, Bryce Canyon, and the Paunsaugunt Plateau.

I stepped out from behind the black mask. Dark clouds hung over the horizon like a plague. I waited. In an instant, the sun broke through a thin white veil. In the time it takes to strike a wooden match, the sun burst, igniting the amphitheater with a pink light that glowed like phosphorous. I could almost hear the light burning. Towering hoodoos lit up like stacks of cordwood stood on end. Wisps of coral clouds drifted across a smudge of powder-blue sky. I was standing in the midst of the strangest, one of the most colorful landscapes I had ever seen, wondering if this was where the Paria River began. And then it was gone. *Pffft!* A wave of ashen clouds smothered the light on the tablelands of the Kaiparowits Plateau.

When Dutton first gazed at the Paunsaugunt Plateau in 1880, he wrote it off, noting it presented "very little matter for special remark." Like many God-fearing folks in these parts, if Dutton wasn't a believer when he first rode into the country he soon converted and trumpeted the word: "The glory of all this rock work is seen in the Pink Cliffs. . . . Standing obelisks, prostrate columns, shattered capitals . . . all bring vividly to mind the suggestions of the work of giant hands, a race of genii now chained up in a spell of enchantment."

What was glorious science for Dutton was "A hell of a place to lose a cow" for Ebenezer Bryce. The Scottish immigrant came to the Paria River Valley with high hopes in 1875. He homesteaded 200 acres near the mouth of Bryce Canyon below the Pink Cliffs. But Bryce and his wife, Mary, were not alone. The valley filled with settlers who

worked their fingers to the bone, and the town of Tropic took root nearby. Bryce and his neighbor Daniel Goulding dug a seven-mile-long canal to irrigate their crops and water their cattle. Upkeep was a fortune. And a drought did them in. Goulding lost 500 fruit trees and moved away. Bryce had no use for the scenery, either. He left the hard, beautiful country that still bears his name and settled in Arizona.

Clouds shadowed me wherever I went. They hung over the east rim of the Paunsaugunt Plateau like a wet carpet. Rain drenched the woodlands, turning it into a bog underfoot. I stuck to the rimlands, and walked through red mud that turned my shoes into skis. Cool moist air turned my breath into steam. I traced the rim as far north as a point called the Fairyland, hoping the clouds would finally break. When gold light poked through a window of blue sky, I could not believe what I saw. Fingers, goblins, hoodoos, pinnacles, and pillars poked out of the foamy pink talus. They looked like totems of reptiles that had been waiting there since time began, bathed in the ancient light of the sun, moon, and sky. To the Paiute they were ancestors turned to stone. That's what a man called "Indian Dick" told park rangers in 1936. "For some reason the people in that place were bad," he said. "Shin-awav turned them all into rocks. You can see them in that place now . . . some standing in rows, some sitting down, some holding onto others. You can see their faces, with paint on them just as they were before they became rocks."

That's what everyone came to see—the rocks. I had, too. But geologists had a different story to tell. Sixty-five million years ago large inland lakes covered southern Utah. Over the millennia the water evaporated, depositing a brilliant geological layer called the Claron Formation. As the region's plateaus began uplifting and faulting ten to fifteen million years ago, the Pink Cliffs weathered and eroded, producing peculiar rock spires surveyors called gnomes, monks, priests, hammers, and temples. Whether the hoodoos were viewed as the souls of ancestors, a maze to track

Hoodoos, the Fairyland

OPPOSITE: *The Sentinel*

Dark cloud silhouette

OPPOSITE: *Silent City*

maverick cattle through, or Queen Victoria herself, there was no denying the mystifying appeal they had on visitors who came from all over the world to see. President Warren G. Harding established Bryce Canyon National Monument on June 8, 1923; five years later, it became a national park.

Weaving through breaks and hoodoos beneath the rim, I still hadn't discovered what I'd set out to find. The one point where I could reach down and dig my fingers into the red rubble, and say this is where the Paria River is born, this is where it begins its journey to reach the mother river one hundred miles away, and who knew how far below. So I drove south along the rim one evening to the place I hoped would be the spot. I wanted to search the ground to the horizon one last time. But thunder and lightning pounded the Pink Cliffs, buffeting my small truck with wind and hammering it with curtains of rain. Visibility was zero. Clouds heavy with moisture clung to the trees, refusing to let go; clouds heavy with condensation clung to the windows, refusing to escape. The day before, a Navajo mechanic fixed the ignition in my truck. He was from "Waaaay over *that* way," he'd said laughing. He told me he drove up here late at night and used his CB radio to talk to his friends, "Waaaay over by Navajo Mount'n." I turned on my truck radio; it crackled with white noise. I turned it off, and sat there listening to the thunder and lightning until the heavens finally parted.

I got out of the truck and watched rivulets of red mud cascade off the cliffs into a hanging canyon. In the distance a rainbow reached down from the clouds and touched the canyon called Paria. The blue dome of Navajo Mountain stood to the north of it. I'd finally found the trail of water that led back home. "Waaaay over *that* way."

Rainbow, Paria Point

Natural Bridge,
Agua Canyon

Sunrise and storm, Kaiparowits Plateau

OPPOSITE: *Hoodoos, The Fairyland*

Wall of Windows

OPPOSITE: *Silent City and the Pink Cliffs*

SIX

CANYONLANDS

Anaasází Dreams

"Here the houses are built into the sides of cliffs . . . evidence that these dreadful cañons were once the homes of families belonging to that great people formerly spread over all this region now so utterly sterile, solitary, and desolate."

—John S. Newberry, 1859
"Labyrinth Cañon"

Tufts of white clouds drifted lazily across the blue sky, the seeds to thunderheads that could deluge the high plateau by late afternoon. It was midmorning, and the air was still cool. For the first time in a week, I hadn't broken a sweat as I walked down a trail that looked like it led to nowhere. For the first time in a week, I wasn't huddling from lightning and rain as I slogged through deep sand toward a butte that looked like a mirage. A collared lizard darted across my path. It ran through the hedge hog that grew along the base of the bluff. In the blink of an eye, it was gone. I followed the tiny claw prints down a trail of rust-colored sand. It led through a carapace of gray soil swarming with life that escaped the naked eye. Leave a careless footprint in the fragile crust of cyanobacteria, and the landscape would be scarred into the next century.

I followed the lizard's trail until it hit a dead end at the foot of the slickrock. I stared up at the wall of petrified sand. It was the last place I would have gone looking for a cliff dwelling. I scrambled up ramps and ledges, zigzagging through cairns that marked the way to the top. I followed a narrow ledge that skirted the rim on the west. It narrowed even more. I reached up and grabbed the rim overhead. I slid my fingers along the rough edges, hoping I wouldn't startle a dozing rattler that might be sleeping off a stomachful of kangaroo rat. I slid my left foot sideways along the ledge, dragging my right foot behind it, careful not to trip over stones that could throw me from the cliff. Sand fell beneath the soles of my feet; a gust of wind blew fine particles of sand back in my face. I edged around the corner, blinking grit out of my eyes until canyon lands yawned before me. The sudden exposure surprised me. I stopped and looked at the boulder that blocked the way beyond. I knocked on it with my knuckles; it didn't sound hollow. So I gripped it like a handle and barn-doored over the edge around it. I planted my feet on the floor of the cave and took a deep breath.

I sat down in silence. Ancient hands had mortared together a small dwelling out of mud and stones in a hollow of the shallow cave. The adobe was big enough to sleep four or five small children, but it was likely a storage granary that held a cache of fire-hardened clay pots filled with seeds, corn, nuts, berries, pemmican, and water. There was enough room outside of it to sleep a family of six or more. I leaned back against the wall of the cave, and sat there struck by the delicate beauty of the cliff dwellers' architecture.

I looked through the mouth of the cave, and the earth met the sky. It dawned on me that the beautiful maze of rimrock and badlands that ushered the Green River through Labyrinth and Stillwater canyons was, indeed, a dreadful place to eke a meager living from the tortured ground. How families survived in such "utterly sterile, solitary, and desolate" country moved me. I had entered a holy place, a shrine to the age of man when life was pared down to the barest necessities, when a family spent every waking hour trying to survive one more day, when a family's worldly possessions could be carried in a single basket suspended by a tumpline, when a family crossed a brutal landscape that waited to eat them alive. I was sitting in a cave that offered refuge from the elements, next to a stone vault that offered hope during famine, at a spot where man crossed over into

PREVIOUS PAGE: *Sunrise, Mesa Arch, Island in the Sky*

OPPOSITE: *Rimrock sunrise, Island in the Sky*

the spirit world. I felt humbled in the presence of a great people that had once spread over the entire region that lay at my feet, and humbled by their power to live in a landscape that modern man could not endure without destroying.

I was held rapt. I did not want to go. I wanted to sit there until the sun went down, and star fire streaked across the dark heavens. I wanted to sit there until the sun came up and the dreams flooded out. I wanted to sit there until the visions could be written on the stones. It would take four days and nights without food and water before the walls began to talk and the spirits began to dance across the rocks. Indigenous people in Mexico still seek such visions by inviting hunger, thirst, and heat. Here, Native peoples had vanished from the face of the land, driven from thousands of potholes that shimmered across the rimrock before mega-droughts scorched the slickrock bare.

Bird pictograph, Cave Spring, The Needles

During his voyage down the Green and Colorado rivers in 1869, Major John Wesley Powell climbed up from the confluence to survey canyon country on July 19. Perched on the rimrock with expedition member George Bradley, Powell described the scene that fell beneath the soles of their boots: "Wherever we look there is but a wilderness of rocks,—deep gorges where the rivers are lost below the cliffs and towers and pinnacles, and ten thousand strangely carved forms in every direction." Wherever I looked out from the cave, I saw that same wilderness of rocks, the same strange "rock forms" Powell wrote "that we do not understand." I did not understand them, either. Where Powell had pondered geology and the future of any civilization that tried to survive west of the one hundredth meridian, I still saw the homelands of ancient peoples who traced their dreams thousands of years into the past. They had left their mark everywhere.

I stared out from the mouth of the cave and remembered a visit to Cave Spring, a line camp in The Needles used by cave-dwelling cowboys for nearly a century. They ate beans, biscuits, and sonuvabitch stew next to an ancient spring that was the only living water for miles around. Just around the corner from where they rolled out their saddle blankets, hand prints had been painted on a ceiling blackened by the smoke of

Hands pictograph, Cave Spring, The Needles

ten thousand campfires. Some of the hand prints were white, outlined with pigment sprayed out of a reed tube. Others were faint orange, painted with the stylized lines of *madi*, East Indian hand tattoos. Were the hand prints personal signatures, as some had speculated, or were they used to call a power from the sacred site? I did not know.

When I was done studying the hands, I looked down, then jumped back. A green snake oozed out of a black hole in the dark wall that dripped with fresh water. There was hardly enough room for the snake to squeeze through, but it did—inch by inch, all four feet of it. The scales sliding over the wet rock sounded like burning kindling. I thought I'd seen everything nature could throw at me, but I'd never seen anything like it before. In the damp, dark overhang, with the sun about to slide into night, it was strange and creepy. I followed the snake along the base of the wall until I noticed the painting of a bird on the ceiling overhead. It had the crude shape of a roadrunner. Archaeologist Polly Schaafsma wrote, "Shamans often claim to be able to engage in flights in which the soul, when it leaves the body, takes the form of a bird." I looked down, and the snake was gone. I had visited with a Paiute woman in Cannonville, Utah, two weeks earlier. I told her about hand prints I'd seen at a waterfall in the Grand Canyon. I asked her what they meant. She told me, long ago her people used to go there when they wanted to cross over into the spirit world.

Nearly everywhere I went in canyon lands, I saw the ancient dreams had been etched and painted on the walls and stones: masks, shamans, medicine men, birthing scenes, clan lines, trails, maps, sandals, bows and arrows, bighorn sheep, centipedes . . . What were the *Anaasází* ("Old Ones") dreaming? I wanted to know. I wanted to dream it. I wanted to see the vision. Yet, everywhere I looked, the ancient dreams were being destroyed—riddled with high-powered rifles (imagine a Picasso being used for target practice?), pried off cliff faces by collectors, chiseled away by religious zealots, spray painted with graffiti, and marred with climbers' chalk. Why were people killing the dreams of the ancestors? I could not fathom it.

Canyonlands National Park, I'd discovered, was an extraordinary region aside. Established by President Lyndon B. Johnson on September 12, 1964, the canyons of the Green and Colorado rivers cleaved the national park's wild geography into thirds. Soaring more than 2,000 feet above the confluence of the Green and Colorado rivers, Island in the Sky offered vistas few early explorers witnessed as they toiled along the Spanish Trail or braved the wild rivers below. Each held me spellbound with aerial views of the La Sal Mountains, White Rim, Monument Canyon, and rivers I'd had the good fortune to row. Cordoned off in the southwest was The Maze, a confusing labyrinth of fins, hoodoos, and canyons thirty miles square. The day before destiny stared me down in Cataract Canyon's Big Drops, I ran wild for hours alone through the solemn beauty of what's been called *the* most remote section of the contiguous United States. Staked down in the southeast corner was The Needles, named for the remarkable color and diversity of its pinnacles and spires. Nestled in a camp surrounded by rocks the shapes of mushrooms, I spent hours scampering across the slickrock with my wife and sons, marveling at a world that existed beyond imagination.

But nothing moved me quite like the cave I was sitting in. This was the spot where man lived on the edge, where a family's future hung in a delicate balance between life and death, feast and famine, culture and extinction. I wanted to sit here until time stood still. I had peace. I had silence. I had no worries. But I also had to go. I was handcuffed to a mechanical timepiece. My civilization no longer trusted the circadian rhythms of the sun, moon, and stars. Closer to home, my own family waited in a near-deserted campground on the edge of the rimrock far below. I crawled out of the cave, tiptoed across the ledge, and ran down the slickrock, still wondering what the *Anaasází* had been dreaming. I followed the trail of collared lizards through the red sand toward the welcome voices of our makeshift canyon home.

OPPOSITE: *Hoodoos, Big Spring Canyon, The Needles*

RIGHT: *Western juniper, Orange Cliffs, Island in the Sky*

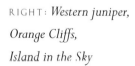

OPPOSITE: *Spirit helpers pictograph, Sego Canyon, Book Cliffs*

LEFT: *Runner, Dead Horse Point*

OPPOSITE: *Summer monsoon, White Rim, Island in the Sky*

Centipedes petroglyph,
Kings Bottom,
Colorado River

Hands pictograph, Cave Spring, The Needles

Fremont cottonwood, Indian Creek

OPPOSITE:

Moonrise, North Six-shooter Peak, Indian Creek

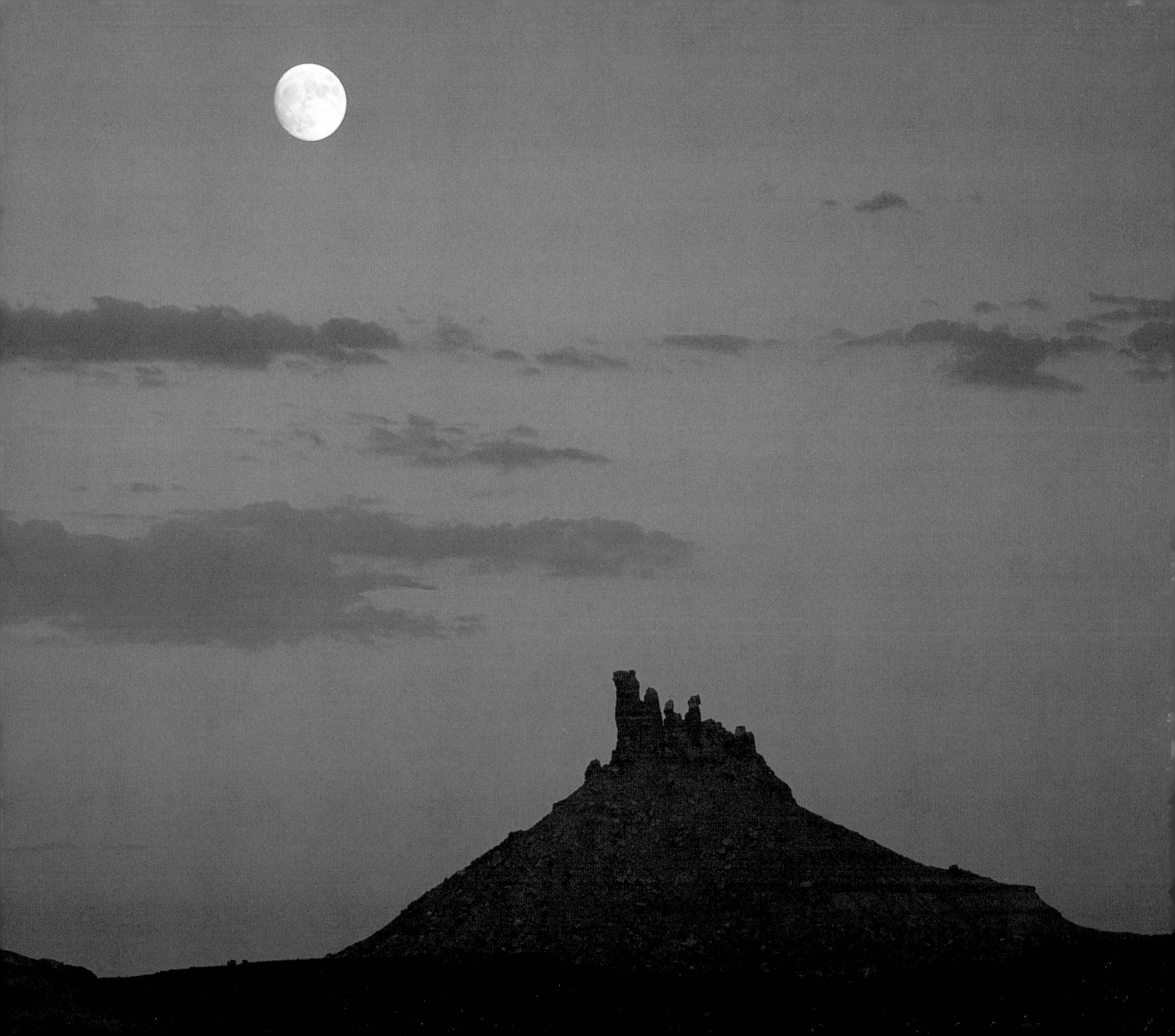

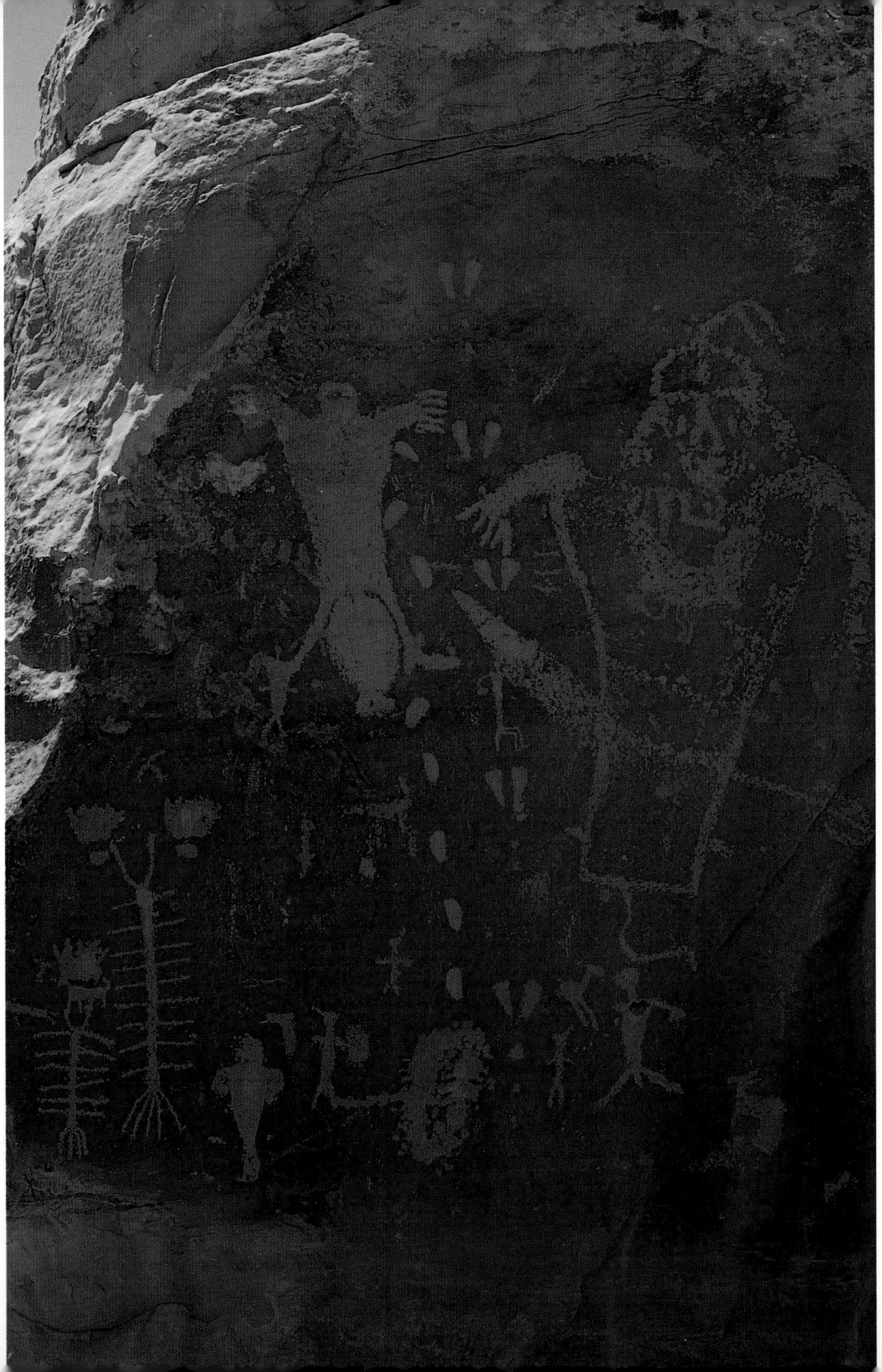

Birthing scene petroglyph,
Kings Bottom,
Colorado River

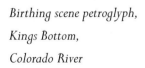

OPPOSITE: *Rimrock, Island in the Sky*

Clan lines petroglyph,
Williams Bottom,
Colorado River

OPPOSITE: *First light, Mesa Arch,*
Island in the Sky

S E V E N

ARCHES

Land of Journeys' Ending

"A weird, lovely, fantastic object out of nature like Delicate Arch
has the curious ability to remind us—like rock and sunlight and wilderness and wind—
that *out there* is a different world, older and greater and deeper by far than ours."
—Edward Abbey, 1968
Desert Solitaire

The warm wind tugged my hair. The August sun bathed my arms. And the white stone cushioned my footfalls. I followed the beaten path as it wound past a log cabin, crossed a wooden footbridge, and climbed out of sight up a wave of Navajo Sandstone. Processions of hikers filed up the ridgeline as far as I could see. Most followed the grooved trail, worn into the soft stone by the scuff marks of who knew how many footsteps. Cairns marked the way for those who found the trail obtuse. I ignored most, scrambling and bounding across the rock, my pace dictated by the rhythm of the stone. The trail wound ever upward, past resilient piñon and juniper that sprouted from crevices slashing the cross-bedded sandstone. I climbed higher, skipping here, twisting there, and enjoying the freedom of movement as I wove through centipedes of legs and boots that climbed up and down the slickrock.

Most had journeyed from all over the United States to pay homage to the one arch in the world against which all others were compared. It beckoned us like moths to light. Hikers scrambling down had Cheshire cat smiles, in contrast to the dogged faces of those still climbing up. Fortunately, there was enough elbow room to keep the westerners among them from getting edgy. We liked our space, about two yards in circumference standing in line at the grocery store. Cross that invisible line and chances are you'd get a "You're not from around here, are you!" look. Things have changed. In 1888, when Civil War veteran John Wesley Wolfe built his cabin at the foot of Delicate Arch, settlers in these parts figured they were getting crowded out if they could see their neighbor's chimney smoke.

I followed the trail over the skyline. It crossed a ledge that had been blasted into the slickrock. Everyone followed this "dugout" past a window-sized arch, and then took seats on a bench of stone overlooking Delicate Arch. I broke away and headed south across the rimrock, hopping from boulder to boulder until I reached a lone reef of rock. I scrambled to the top and sat down. Beneath me was Delicate Arch. Called "The Chaps" and the "Schoolmarm's Bloomers" by Moab cowboys in the 1880s, it sat high on a stone bluff at the west end of a line of domes that stood 500 feet above the braid of arroyos called Winter Camp Wash, Cache Valley Wash, and Salt Wash. Cowboys who still ran cattle through the area in 1935 had a simple answer for such beautiful desolation when eastern photographer Harry Reid came calling: "They wa'ant nothin' out there. Jest a lot of holes in rocks." That's were I was sitting, *out there*, across the divide from a hundred or more people who had also come here to get away from it all. They gathered to watch sunset and snap photos of one another standing beneath a picture frame of stone forty-five feet high and thirty-three feet wide. I sat on the perch alone, transfixed by the raw pink stone.

When author Edward Abbey first eyed Delicate Arch one windy day in May nearly a half century ago, he lived in a trailer near Balanced Rock at the end of a dirt road that led from the cattle, potash, and uranium boomtown of Moab. He drove his government pickup to Wolfe's Cabin and homestead on Salt Wash at the foot of the slickrock called the Bar-DX Ranch. Abbey, whom I saw one hot September night at a gathering of local desert rats, had the gait of a tall Texan. Sitting on my perch, I could only

PREVIOUS PAGE: *Delicate Arch*

Balanced Rock,
The Windows

imagine him striding up the slickrock to see Delicate Arch. He was the lone ranger in these parts, who spent a season in this wilderness. He wrote an epiphany that was both a paean and an elegy to the place. Words from his memories had brought me here, once again: "Between here and there and me and the mountains is the canyon wilderness, the hoodoo land of spire and pillar and pinnacle where no man lives, and where the river flows, unseen." In his seminal book, *Desert Solitaire*, he also wrote, "After Delicate Arch, the others are anticlimactic but I go on to inspect them, as I'm paid to do."

Abbey was right about Delicate Arch. At the time, ninety arches had been discovered in the monument. Since then more than 2,000 arches have been cataloged in the park, from 3-foot-wide windows to 306-foot spans. Why here? Geologists tell us that 300 million years ago ocean waters that once covered the area retreated, depositing a bed of salt. Over the millennia, the earth's crust compressed and faulted, thrusting marvelously colored fins of rock skyward. Carbon dioxide from organic matter, rain, and snow dissolved the natural cement that glued the Entrada Sandstone fins together. Alcoves formed in the thin walls, and arches began forming when water, wind, and gravity carried away enough sand.

That's what everyone had come to see. I had, too. That's why President Herbert Hoover established Arches National Monument on April 12, 1929, and President Lyndon B. Johnson enlarged the area into a national park on January 20, 1969. But this was the West, the land of bait and switch, and swimming pools in the sand. If you came to see a river, there was a fair chance you'd see a dry gulch. If you came to see a lake, there was a fair chance you'd see a mirage. If you came to see a canyon, there was a fair chance you'd see a monument. Arches National Park was no different. I'd come to see its arches, but I was surprised to discover its gardens of stone.

To the north was Devils Garden: I followed narrow corridors pinched between slickrock walls to see Landscape Arch (the longest in the park at 306 feet wall-to-wall), but I discovered towering fins, pillars, domes, and dollops of sand awash in the pink

OPPOSITE: *Fins, Devils Garden*

light of daybreak. To the west was the Fiery Furnace: I traced a maze of ledges, blind alleys, and dead ends through monsoon gloom and darkness to see Surprise Arch, one of the most hidden in the park, but I discovered a black lightning rod of stone that poked out of look-alike terrain that pioneer cowboys called "slickrock corrals." To the south were The Windows: I climbed up a drift of hot sand to see Double Arch, the most remarkable in the park for its double span, but I discovered the Garden of Eden's golden goblins of stone. Farther south were Courthouse Towers: I'd gone there to see Baby Arch, one of the smallest in the park (twenty-five feet wide), but I discovered an uncanny setting straight out of Monument Valley. And to the northwest were the Klondike Bluffs: I'd never been there, but from where I sat, I watched the sun plummet behind a veil of gray clouds, streaked with firebrands of red light.

Tree, last light, Devils Garden

OPPOSITE: *"Monument Valley," Park Avenue*

From my perch, I watched wisps of white virga fall through shafts of sunlight that poked through soft, steel-blue clouds, cascading through tufts of dusty-blue and flaxen light that shrouded the black folds of the rimrock. I watched the cloud-covered sky go from blue to orange, to red, to purple, then black. I watched drifts of fuchsia and damson paint Delicate Arch yellow, gold, pink, then vermilion. I sat there in silence until dark.

Night fell as I hopped from boulder to boulder. The sun had set a half hour earlier, but there was still a half hour of dim light remaining before I needed to turn on my flashlight. I danced down the slickrock with carefree abandon. I was happy. The Milky Way started to light up the black sky, and, as my eyes adjusted, I could almost see clear as day. This was the end trail for me. But it was also the beginning. This was where I'd made my first journey through the canyons, mesas, and slickrock country of the high plateaus

more than fifteen years ago. This journey had been no less compelling. I had been blessed to see country many eyes have still not seen. I'd had the good fortune to follow trails that still lead deep into the time of legend. And I had been touched by spirits Native peoples believe still dwell here.

Floating in the darkness, the wind at my back, the ground rising up to meet me, the words of a Navajo prayer came back to me; they were from *The Night Chant*:

In beauty I walk
With beauty before me I walk
With beauty behind me I walk
With beauty above me I walk
With beauty above and
about me I walk
It is finished in beauty
It is finished in beauty.

In darkness and beauty I had finished my journey.

Sand Dune Arch,
Devils Garden

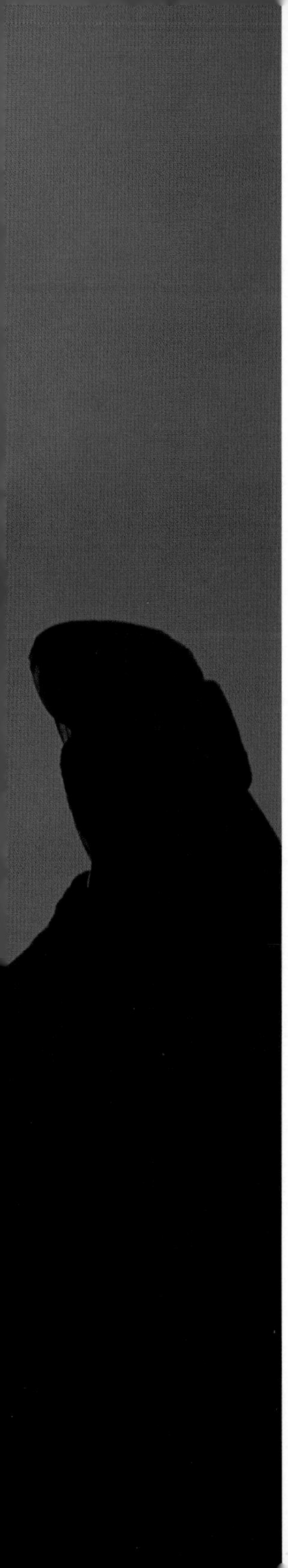

LEFT: *Spires, Fiery Furnace*

OPPOSITE: *Nefertittis Head, Park Avenue*

Garden of Eden, The Windows

Three Gossips, Park Avenue

Domes, Devils Garden

OPPOSITE: *Tower of Babel, Courthouse Towers*

Nefertittis Head, Park Avenue

OPPOSITE: *Candelabrum, Park Avenue*

Nightfall, Courthouse Towers

OPPOSITE: *Sunset, Klondike Bluffs*

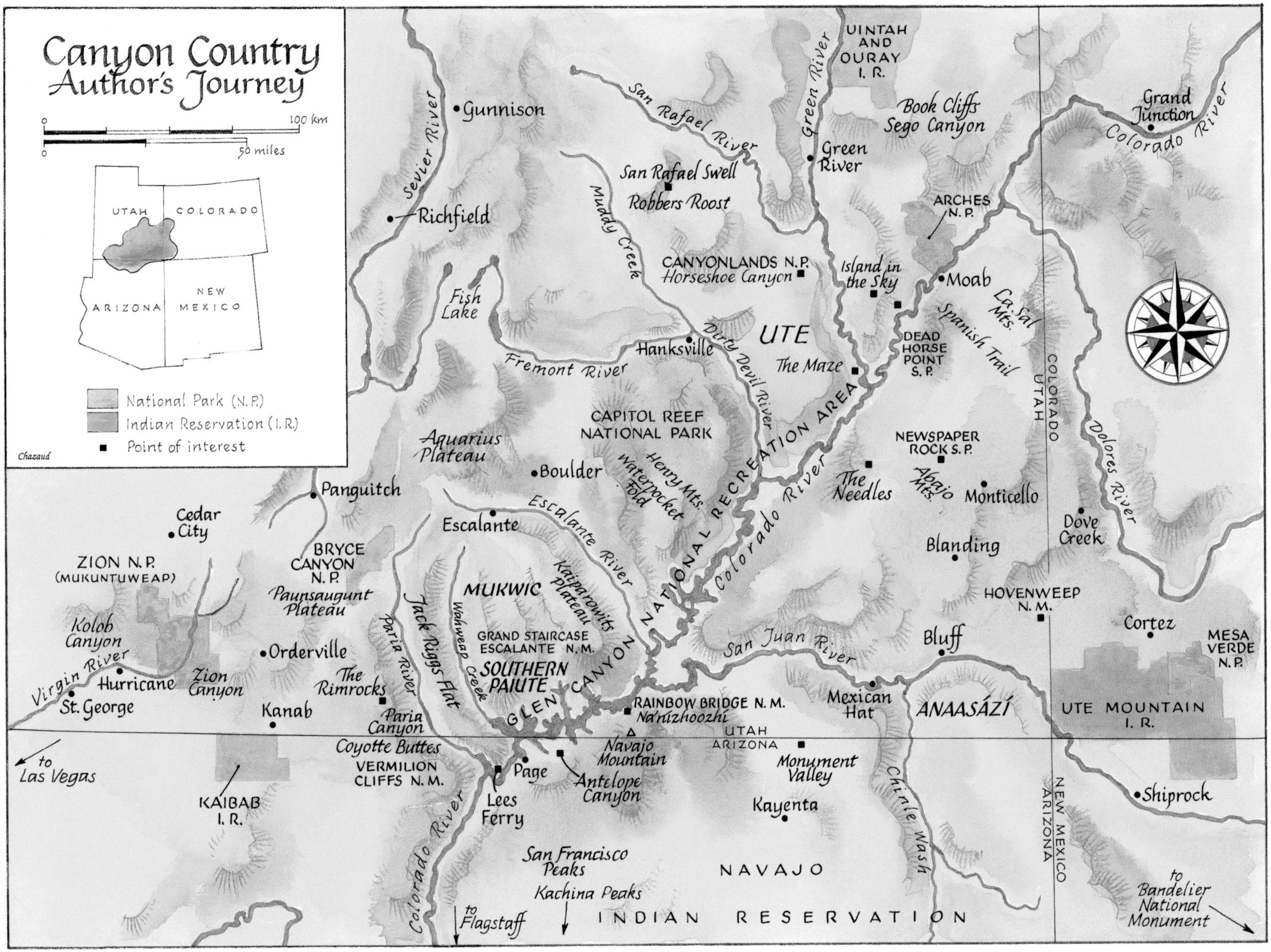

Canyon Country
Author's Journey
0
100 km
0
50 miles
UTAH
COLORADO
ARIZONA
NEW MEXICO
National Park (N.P.)
Indian Reservation (I.R.)
Point of interest
Chazaud
Gunnison
Sevier River
Richfield
San Rafael River
San Rafael Swell
Robbers Roost
Muddy Creek
Green River
Green River
UINTAH AND OURAY I.R.
Book Cliffs
Sego Canyon
Grand Junction
Colorado River
ARCHES N.P.
CANYONLANDS N.P.
Horseshoe Canyon
Island in the Sky
Moab
La Sal Mts.
Spanish Trail
Fish Lake
Hanksville
Dirty Devil River
UTE
The Maze
DEAD HORSE POINT S.P.
Fremont River
CAPITOL REEF NATIONAL PARK
Aquarius Plateau
Boulder
Henry Mts.
Waterpocket Fold
GLEN CANYON NATIONAL RECREATION AREA
Colorado River
NEWSPAPER ROCK S.P.
The Needles
Abajo Mts.
Monticello
COLORADO
UTAH
Dolores River
Dove Creek
Panguitch
Cedar City
Escalante
Escalante River
Blanding
ZION N.P. (MUKUNTUWEAP)
BRYCE CANYON N.P.
Paunsaugunt Plateau
MUKWIC
Kaiparowits Plateau
HOVENWEEP N.M.
Cortez
Kolob Canyon
Orderville
Paria River
Jack Riggs Flat
Wahweap Creek
GRAND STAIRCASE ESCALANTE N.M.
SOUTHERN PAIUTE
San Juan River
Bluff
MESA VERDE N.P.
Virgin River
Hurricane
Zion Canyon
St. George
The Rimrocks
Kanab
Paria Canyon
RAINBOW BRIDGE N.M.
Na'nízhoozhí
Mexican Hat
ANAASÁZÍ
UTE MOUNTAIN I.R.
to Las Vegas
Coyotte Buttes
VERMILION CLIFFS N.M.
Page
Navajo Mountain
UTAH
ARIZONA
Monument Valley
Antelope Canyon
Lees Ferry
KAIBAB I.R.
Kayenta
Chinle Wash
Shiprock
NEW MEXICO
ARIZONA
Colorado River
San Francisco Peaks
NAVAJO
Kachina Peaks
to Flagstaff
INDIAN RESERVATION
to Bandelier National Monument

SELECTED BIBLIOGRAPHY

Abbey, Edward. *Desert Solitaire: A Season in the Wilderness.* New York: Ballantine Books, 1968.

____. *Slickrock: Endangered Canyons of the Southwest* (photographs and commentary by Philip Hyde). New York: Sierra Club/Charles Scribner's Sons, 1971.

Annerino, John. *Grand Canyon Wild: A Photographic Journey* (photographs by the author). Woodstock, VT: Countryman Press, 2004.

____. *Canyons of the Southwest: A Tour of the Great Canyon Country from Colorado to Northern Mexico* (photographs by the author), cloth. San Francisco: Sierra Club Books, 1993. University of Arizona Press paperback edition, 2000.

____. *People of Legend: Native Americans of the Southwest* (photographs by the author). San Francisco: Sierra Club Books, 1996.

____. "Four Sacred Mountains" (photographs by the author). *The Navajo Times, America's Largest Indian Weekly*, vol. 24, no. 32 (August 12, 1982): 14.

____. "Sacred Mountains of the Navajo" (photographs by the author). *Arizona, The Arizona Republic Magazine*, May 9, 1982: cover, 6–8.

Beidleman, Robert G. "The Black Canyon of the Gunnison National Monument." *Colorado Magazine* (State Historical Society of Colorado), vol. 40, no. 3 (July 1963): 161–78.

Bernheimer, Charles L. *Rainbow Bridge: Circling Navajo Mountain and Explorations in the "Bad Lands" of Southern Utah and Northern Arizona* (illustrations from photographs). Garden City and New York: Doubleday, Page & Company, 1926.

Bolton, Herbert E. *Pageant in the Wilderness: The Story of the Escalante Expedition to the Interior Basin, 1776, Including the Diary and Itinerary of Father Escalante, Translated and Annotated.* Salt Lake City: Utah Historical Society, 1950.

Callaway, Donald, Joel Janetski, and Omer C. Stewart. "Ute." In *Handbook of North American Indians.* Vol. 11, *Great Basin.* Washington, DC: Smithsonian Institution, 1986.

Cordell, Linda S. "Prehistory: Eastern Anasazi." In *Handbook of North American Indians.* Vol. 9, *Southwest.* Washington, DC: Smithsonian Institution, 1979.

Crampton, C. Gregory. *Land of Living Rock: The Grand Canyon and the High Plateaus: Arizona, Utah, Nevada.* New York: Alfred A. Knopf, 1972.

____. *Standing Up Country: The Canyon Lands of Utah and Arizona.* New York and Salt Lake City: Alfred A. Knopf and University of Utah Press, in Association with the Amon Carter Museum of Western Art, 1964.

Dellenbaugh, Frederick S. *A Canyon Voyage: The Narrative of the Second Powell Expedition Down the Green-Colorado River from Wyoming, and the Explorations on Land, in the Years, 1871 and 1872.* New York and London: G. P. Putnam's Sons, 1908.

____. *Romance of the Colorado River: The Story of Its Discovery in 1540, with an Account of the Later Explorations, and with Special Reference to the Voyages of Powell Through the Line of Great Canyons.* New York and London: G. P. Putnam's Sons, 1902.

Dutton, Clarence E. *Teritary History of the Grand Cañon District, With Atlas.* Washington: Government Printing Office, 1882. p. 57.

Flog, Fred. "Prehistory: Western Anasazi." In *Handbook of North American Indians*. Vol. 9, *Southwest*. Washington, DC: Smithsonian Institution, 1979.

Gannett, Henry. *A Gazetteer of Utah*. Geological Survey Bulletin 166. Washington, DC: U.S. Government Printing Office, 1900.

Gregory, Herbert E. *A Geologic and Geographic Sketch of Zion and Bryce National Parks.* Springdale, UT: Zion-Bryce Natural History Association, 1956.

———. *Colorado Plateau Region.* International Geological Congress XVI Session. Washington, DC: U.S. Government Printing Office, 1932.

———. *The Geology and Geography of the Paunsaugunt Region Utah: A Survey of Parts of Garfield and Kane Counties.* Geological Professional Paper 226. Washington, DC: U.S. Government Printing Office, 1951.

———. *Geology and Geography of the Zion Park Region Utah and Arizona: A Comprehensive Report on a Scenic and Historic Region of the Southwest.* Geological Survey Professional Paper 220. Washington, DC: U.S. Government Printing Office, 1950.

Gregory, Herbert E., and J. C. Anderson. "Geographic and Geologic Sketch of the Capitol Reef Region of Utah." *Bulletin of the Geological Society of America*, vol. 50 (December 1939): 1827–50.

Gregory, Herbert E., and Robert C. Moore. *The Kaiparowits Region: A Geographic and Geologic Reconnaissance of Utah and Arizona.* U.S. Department of the Interior Professional Paper 164. Washington, DC: U.S. Government Printing Office, 1931.

Grey, Zane. *Tales of Lonely Trails.* New York and London: Harper & Brothers, 1922.

Horan, James D. *Desperate Men: The James Gang and the Wild Bunch.* Lincoln: University of Nebraska Press, Bison Books, 1997. First published by Doubleday, New York, 1949.

James, George Wharton. *Utah: The Land of Blossoming Valleys.* Boston: Page Company, 1922.

Kelly, Charles. "The Mysterious 'D. Julian.'" *Utah Historical Quarterly*, vol. 6, no. 3 (July 1933): 83–88.

Kelly, Isabel T. "Southern Paiute Ethnography." University of Utah, Anthropological Papers, no. 69 (May 1964). Glen Canyon Series 21.

Kelly, Isabel T., and Catherine S. Fowler. "Southern Paiute." In *Handbook of North American Indians.* Vol. 11, *Great Basin.* Washington, DC: Smithsonian Institution, 1986.

Knipmeyer, James H. *Butch Cassidy Was Here: Historic Inscriptions of the Colorado Plateau* (photographs by the author). Salt Lake City: University of Utah Press, 2002.

Kolb, Ellsworth L. *Through the Grand Canyon from Wyoming to Mexico.* New York: MacMillan, 1914.

Lacy, Hugh. "Say That I Kept My Dream." *The Desert Magazine*, vol. 1, no. 11 (September 1938): 18–20.

Lee, Katie. *All My Rivers Are Gone.* Boulder, CO: Johnson Books, 1998.

Linford, Laurance D. *Navajo Places: History, Legend, Landscape.* Salt Lake City: University of Utah Press, 2000.

Luckert, Karl W. *Navajo Mountain and Rainbow Bridge Religion.* Flagstaff, AZ: Museum of Northern Arizona, 1977.

Macomb, J. N. *Report of the Exploring Expedition from Sante Fé, New Mexico, to the Junction of the Grand and Green Rivers of the Great Colorado of the West, in 1859, Under the Command of Capt. J. N. Macomb; with a Geological Report by Prof. J. S. Newberry.* Washington, DC: Government Printing Office, 1876.

Matthews, Washington. *The Night Chant, A Navaho Ceremony.* New York: Memoirs of the American Museum of Natural History, 1902.

Mooney, James. "The Ghost Dance Religion and the Sioux Outbreak of 1890." In *Fourteenth Annual Report of the Bureau of Ethnology, 1892–93* by J. W. Powell, Part 2. Washington, DC: Government Printing Office, 1896.

Nichols, Tad. *Glen Canyon: Images of a Lost World* (photographs by the author). Santa Fe: Museum of New Mexico Press, 1999.

Palmer, William R. "The Pahute Fire Legend." *Utah Historical Quarterly*, vol. 6, no. 2 (April 1933): 62–64.

———. "Indian Names in Utah Geography." *Utah Historical Quarterly*, vol. 1, no. 1 (January 1928): 5, 12–13, 16–17.

———. "Utah Indians Past and Present: An Etymological and Historical Study of Tribes and Tribal Names from Original Sources by Wm. R. Palmer, Cedar City, Utah." *Utah Historical Quarterly*, vol. 1, no. 1 (April 1928).

Peattie, Roderick, editor. *The Inverted Mountains: Canyons of the West* (contributors Harold S. Colton, Weldon F. Heald, Edwin D. McKee). New York: Vanguard Press, 1948.

Porter, Eliot. *The Place No One Knew: Glen Canyon on the Colorado* (edited by David Brower). San Francisco: Sierra Club Books, 1963.

Powell, J. W. *Report on the Arid Lands of the United States, with a More Detailed Account of the Lands of Utah*. Second edition. Washington, DC: Government Printing Office, 1879.

____. *Exploration of the Colorado River of the West and Its Tributaries. Explored in 1869, 1870, 1871, and 1872, Under the Direction of the Secretary of the Smithsonian Institution.* Washington, DC: Government Printing Office, 1875.

Reichard, Gladys A. *Navajo Religion: A Study in Symbolism.* Bollingen Series 18. Princeton, NJ: Princeton University Press, 1963.

Reisner, Marc. *Cadillac Desert: The American West and Its Disappearing Water.* New York: Penguin Books, 1986.

Roessel, Robert A., Jr. "Navajo History, 1850–1923." In *Handbook of North American Indians.* Vol. 10, *Southwest*. Washington, DC: Smithsonian Institution, 1983.

Rowell, Galen. *High & Wild: Essays and Photographs on Wilderness Adventure* (photographs by the author, introduction by Robert Redford). Bishop, CA: Spotted Dog Press, 2002.

Ruess, Everett. *On Desert Trails with Everett Ruess* (introduction by Hugh Lacy, foreword by Randall Henderson, afterword by Gary James Bergera, and epilogue by W. L. Rusho). Salt Lake City: Gibbs Smith Publishers, 2000.

Schaafsma, Polly. *Tse Yaa Kin: Houses Beneath the Rock*, edited by David Grant Noble. Santa Fe, NM: School of American Research, 1986.

Smith, Fred. J., Jr., Lymun C. Huff, E. Neal Hinrichs, and Robert C. Luedke. *Geology of the Capitol Reef Area, Wayne and Garfield Counties, Utah, Prepared on Behalf of the U.S. Atomic Energy Commission.* Geological Survey Professional Paper 363. Washington, DC: U.S. Government Printing Office, 1963.

Stevens, Dale John, and J. Edward McCarrick. *The Arches of Arches National Park: A Comprehensive Study.* Orem, UT: Mainstay Publishing, 1988.

Thompson, A. H. "Report on a Trip to the Mouth of the Dirty Devil River." In *Exploration of the Colorado River of the West and Its Tributaries. Explored in 1869, 1870, 1871, and 1872* by J. W. Powell. Washington, DC: Government Printing Office, 1875.

Van Valkenberg, Richard F., and Clyde Kluckhorn, eds. *Navajo Indians III: Navajo Sacred Places*. New York: Garland Publishing, 1974.

Woodbury, Angus M. "A History of Southern Utah and Its National Parks." *Utah State Historical Quarterly*, vol. 12, nos. 3–4 (July–October 1944): 111–224. Revised and reprinted in 1950.

Workers of the Writers' Program of the Works Progress Administration for the State of Utah, comp. *Utah: Guide to the State*. New York: Hastings House, 1941.

PAGE 138: *Hands pictograph, Cave Spring, The Needles*

LITERATURE CITED

p. 5. "Whenever he went out by himself, he heard the songs of spirits"; Washington Matthews. *The Night Chant, A Navaho Ceremony*. New York: Memoirs of the American Museum of Natural History, 1902, p. 159.

p. 9. "We have lived upon this land from the days beyond history's record"; John Annerino. *Canyons of the Southwest*. San Francisco: Sierra Club Books, 1993, p. 139.

p. 10. "Is this the only canyon? Are there others?"; C. Gregory Crampton. *Standing Up Country: The Canyon Lands of Utah and Arizona*. New York: Alfred A. Knopf, 1964, p. vii.

p. 13. "Tenderfoot and cliff-dweller from Manhattan"; Charles L. Bernheimer. *Rainbow Bridge: Circling Navajo Mountain in the "Bad Lands" of Southern Utah and Northern Arizona.* Garden City and New York: Doubleday, Page & Company, 1926, p. xi.

p. 13. "one of the most inspiring marvels of the ages"; Bernheimer, p. 78.

p. 15. "It was not for many eyes to see"; Zane Grey. *Tales of Lonely Trails.* New York and London: Harper & Brothers, 1922, p. 17.

p. 17. "From one rim of the Grand Canyon, you can easily see"; Crampton, pp. 8, 12.

p. 18. "An independent cuss . . . and two-fisted drinker"; Marc Reisner. *Cadillac Desert: The American West and Its Disappearing Water*. New York: Penguin Books, 1986, pp. 223, 240.

p. 22. "There is as much country standing up as there is laying down"; Crampton, p. 16.

p. 33. "I am exploring southward to the Colorado, where no one lives"; Everett Ruess. *On Desert Trails with Everett Ruess.* Salt Lake City: Gibbs Smith Publishers, 2000, p. 106.

p. 33. "seemed more beautiful to me than ever before"; Ruess, p. 8.

p. 34. "The country between here and the San Juan and Colorado rivers"; Ruess, p. 45.

p. 36. "The region is desolate and abandoned even by the Indians"; Herbert E. Gregory and Raymond C. Moore. *The Kaiparowits Region: A Geographic and Geologic Reconnaissance of Parts of Utah and Arizona.* U.S. Geological Survey Professional Paper 164. Washington, DC: U.S. Government Printing Office, 1931, p. 6.

p. 37. "A large portion of this area is"; A. H. Thompson. "Report on a Trip to the Mouth of the Dirty Devil River" in *Exploration of the Colorado River of the West and Its Tributaries. Explored in 1869, 1870, 1871, and 1872* by J. W. Powell. Washington, DC: Government Printing Office, 1875, pp. 137–38.

p. 38. "vanished—into thin air"; Hugh Lacy in *On Desert Trails with Everett Ruess*, p. xi.

p. 38. "Sunset made all the misery worth enduring"; Ruess, p. 14.

p. 49. "In some places the holes are so deep that we have to swim"; J. W. Powell. *Exploration of the Colorado River of the West and Its Tributaries. Explored in 1869, 1870, 1871, and 1872.* Washington, DC: Government Printing Office, 1875, pp. 109–10.

p. 50. "Wading again this morning; sinking in the quicksand"; Powell, p. 110.

p. 50. "it was not Zion"; Angus M. Woodbury. "A History of Southern Utah and Its National Parks." *Utah State Historical Quarterly*, vol. 12, nos. 3–4 (July–October 1944): p 158.

p. 54. "When the sun died, I went up to heaven"; James Mooney. "The Ghost Dance Religion and the Sioux Outbreak of 1890." *Fourteenth Annual Report of the Bureau of Ethnology, 1892–93*, J. W. Powell, Part 2. Washington, DC: Government Printing Office, 1896, p. 746.

p. 54. "In an instant there flashed before us a scene"; Clarence E. Dutton. *Teritary History of the Grand Cañon District, With Atlas.* Washington: Government Printing Office, 1882. P. 57.

p. 55. "brick standing on end"; Galen Rowell. *High & Wild: Essays and*

Photographs on Wilderness Adventure. Bishop, CA: Spotted Dog Press, 2002, p. 46.

p. 55. "The full moon was shining into the depths of the canyon"; Woodbury, p. 163.

p. 65. "No place left to hide. Violent death had thinned the ranks of the . . . Wild Bunch"; James D. Horan. *Desperate Men: The James Gang and the Wild Bunch*. Lincoln: University of Nebraska Press, Bison Books, 1997, p. 263.

p. 66. "she could ride like a Sioux wind"; Horan, p. 192.

p. 69. "the second great god of the Paiutes"; William R. Palmer. "The Pahute Fire Legend." *Utah Historical Quarterly*, vol. 6, no. 2 (April 1933), p. 62.

p. 70. "It is useless"; Palmer, p. 62.

p. 83. "It's a hell of a place to lose a cow"; Crampton, p. 116.

p. 85. "As one old-timer expressed it, they were far from home, looking"; Herbert E. Gregory. *The Geology and Geography of the Paunsaugunt Region, Utah: A Survey of Parts of Garfield and Kane Counties*. Geological Survey Professional Paper 226. Washington, DC: U.S. Government Printing Office, 1951, p. 4.

p. 85. "The glory of all this rock work is seen in the Pink Cliffs"; Dutton, p. 254.

p. 87. "For some reason the people in that place were bad"; Gregory, p. 17.

p. 87. "Here the houses are built in the sides of cliffs"; John S. Newberry in *Report of the Exploring Expedition from Santa Fé, New Mexico, to the Junction of the Grand and Green rivers of the Great Colorado of the West, in 1859, Under the Command of Capt. J. N. Macomb; with a Geological Report by Prof. J. S. Newberry*. Washington, DC: Government Printing Office, 1876, p. 95.

p. 100. "Wherever we look there is but a wilderness of rocks"; Powell, p. 213.

p. 100. "rock forms that we do not understand"; Powell, p. 212.

p. 101. "Shamans often claim to be able to engage in flights"; Polly Schaafsma. *Tse Yaa Kin: Houses Beneath the Rock*, edited by David Grant Noble. Sante Fe, NM: School of American Research, 1986, p. 194.

p. 117. "A weird, lovely, fantastic object out of nature like Delicate Arch has"; Edward Abbey. *Desert Solitaire: A Season in the Wilderness*. New York: Ballantine Books, 1968, pp. 41–42.

p. 121. "Between here and there and me and the mountains"; Abbey, p. 218.

p. 121. "After Delicate Arch, the others are anticlimactic"; Abbey, p. 42.

p. 124. "In beauty I walk . . . it is finished in beauty"; Matthews, pp. 143–45.